HOUGHTON MIFFLIN

math CENTRAL

Daily Cumulative Review

Level 5

HOUGHTON MIFFLIN

Boston • Atlanta • Dallas • Denver • Geneva, Illinois • Palo Alto • Princeton

DAILY CUMULATIVE REVIEW

Write the answer.

1. 0 + 2	**2.** 6 − 1	**3.** 9 + 3	**4.** 7 − 2
5. 7 + 5	**6.** 5 − 3	**7.** 7 + 3	**8.** 15 − 7
9. 9 + 9	**10.** 8 + 2	**11.** 15 − 6	**12.** 10 − 3
13. 7 + 4	**14.** 8 + 3	**15.** 13 − 6	**16.** 17 − 9

Solve.

17. Billy put together 3 model airplanes during his summer vacation. He already had 5 model airplanes. How many model airplanes does he have in all? _____

18. Mrs. Roberts donated 16 jars of peach jam to sell at the school fair. At the end of the fair 2 jars were left. How many jars were sold? _____

Name _____

2 DAILY CUMULATIVE REVIEW

Write the answer.

1. 14
   + 10

2. 28
   − 8

3. 15
   + 14

4. 25
   + 8

5. 26
   − 13

6. 17
   − 11

7. 37
   + 29

8. 48
   − 17

Write the number in standard form.

9. ten _____

10. twenty-four _____

11. sixty-two _____

12. one hundred thirty _____

13. two hundred _____

14. five hundred six _____

Solve.

15. Rebecca read 15 books during the summer and Sarah read 22 books. How many books did they read in all during the summer?

_____

3 DAILY CUMULATIVE REVIEW

Write the answer.

1.	2.	3.	4.
52 + 40	23 + 31	61 − 50	59 − 16

5.	6.	7.	8.
72 + 24	27 − 12	48 − 35	56 + 32

Write the numbers in order from least to greatest.

9. 20, 23, 32, 16   _____

10. 45, 86, 84, 47   _____

11. 110, 120, 102, 112   _____

12. 690, 670, 607, 699   _____

13. 152, 51, 261, 37   _____

14. 190, 90, 119, 19   _____

Solve.

15. Amado gave his mother a bouquet of 6 daisies, 4 carnations, and 2 roses. How many flowers did Amado give his mother?

_____

Name _____

 4 **DAILY CUMULATIVE REVIEW**

Write the answer.

1. $\begin{array}{r} 7 \\ + 4 \\ \hline \end{array}$
    2. $\begin{array}{r} 5 \\ + 9 \\ \hline \end{array}$
    3. $\begin{array}{r} 8 \\ - 3 \\ \hline \end{array}$
    4. $\begin{array}{r} 14 \\ - 7 \\ \hline \end{array}$

5. $\begin{array}{r} 8 \\ + 8 \\ \hline \end{array}$
    6. $\begin{array}{r} 17 \\ - 9 \\ \hline \end{array}$
    7. $\begin{array}{r} 8 \\ + 4 \\ \hline \end{array}$
    8. $\begin{array}{r} 16 \\ - 9 \\ \hline \end{array}$

9. $\begin{array}{r} 6 \\ + 6 \\ \hline \end{array}$
    10. $\begin{array}{r} 11 \\ - 2 \\ \hline \end{array}$
    11. $\begin{array}{r} 15 \\ - 7 \\ \hline \end{array}$
    12. $\begin{array}{r} 5 \\ + 5 \\ \hline \end{array}$

Solve.

13. Mrs. Branner baked 6 cherry and
    2 strawberry pies one afternoon.
    How many pies did she bake in all?

    _____

14. A cheetah's top speed is 70 miles per hour.
    A giraffe's top speed is 32 miles per hour.
    How much faster is the cheetah's top speed
    than the giraffe's?

    _____

Name _____

5 DAILY CUMULATIVE REVIEW

Write the answer.

1. 40
   + 11

2. 179
   – 67

3. 81
   + 13

4. 48
   – 20

5. 806
   + 193

6. 784
   – 270

7. 462
   + 315

8. 538
   – 223

Write the digit in the tens place.

9. 596 _____

10. 601 _____

11. 480 _____

12. 123 _____

Write the digit in the hundreds place.

13. 186 _____

14. 283 _____

15. 5740 _____

16. 8026 _____

Solve.

17. Mary raised chickens for her 4-H project. After
   she sold 21 chickens, she had 12 left. How
   many chickens did she raise in all?

   _____

Name _____

Write the answer.

1. 83 + 61	**2.** 58 + 12	**3.** 72 − 16	**4.** 61 − 38
5. 47 − 29	**6.** 87 + 59	**7.** 65 + 78	**8.** 90 − 42

Compare. Write < or >.

9. 30 ◯ 50   **10.** 212 ◯ 208

11. 312 ◯ 231   **12.** 747 ◯ 774

13. 606 ◯ 607   **14.** 350 ◯ 305

15. 62 ◯ 426   **16.** 452 ◯ 542

Solve.

17. Paula paid $5 to rent a space at the swap meet. She sold old toys and clothes for a total of $35. How much money did she make after she subtracted the cost of renting the space?

_____

7 **DAILY CUMULATIVE REVIEW**

Write the answer.

1. $\begin{array}{r} 19 \\ -\ 9 \\ \hline \end{array}$	**2.** $\begin{array}{r} 13 \\ +\ 2 \\ \hline \end{array}$	**3.** $\begin{array}{r} 12 \\ -\ 8 \\ \hline \end{array}$	**4.** $\begin{array}{r} 9 \\ +\ 9 \\ \hline \end{array}$
5. $\begin{array}{r} 5 \\ +\ 6 \\ \hline \end{array}$	**6.** $\begin{array}{r} 7 \\ +\ 7 \\ \hline \end{array}$	**7.** $\begin{array}{r} 17 \\ -\ 7 \\ \hline \end{array}$	**8.** $\begin{array}{r} 15 \\ -\ 9 \\ \hline \end{array}$
9. $\begin{array}{r} 7 \\ +\ 0 \\ \hline \end{array}$	**10.** $\begin{array}{r} 9 \\ -\ 5 \\ \hline \end{array}$	**11.** $\begin{array}{r} 15 \\ -\ 10 \\ \hline \end{array}$	**12.** $\begin{array}{r} 9 \\ +\ 4 \\ \hline \end{array}$
13. $\begin{array}{r} 8 \\ +\ 7 \\ \hline \end{array}$	**14.** $\begin{array}{r} 5 \\ -\ 5 \\ \hline \end{array}$	**15.** $\begin{array}{r} 16 \\ -\ 7 \\ \hline \end{array}$	**16.** $\begin{array}{r} 9 \\ -\ 3 \\ \hline \end{array}$

Solve.

17. The bicycle was invented in 1816 and the camera was invented in 1822. Which was invented first?

_____

18. Sue Ann bicycled 12 miles in the morning and 9 miles in the afternoon. How far did she bicycle in all?

_____

Name _____

 8 DAILY CUMULATIVE REVIEW

Write the answer.

1.	50 + 25	**2.**	125 − 10	**3.**	71 + 38

4.	608 − 402	**5.**	65 + 32	**6.**	181 − 60

7.	47 + 82	**8.**	439 − 105	**9.**	256 − 30

Compare. Write < or >.

10. 95 ◯ 51   **11.** 216 ◯ 217

12. 373 ◯ 337   **13.** 1435 ◯ 1453

14. 585 ◯ 855   **15.** 9843 ◯ 9384

16. 2341 ◯ 3214   **17.** 807 ◯ 808

Solve.

18. Mrs. Hom is 35 years old. Her son is 21 years younger than she is. How old is her son?

_____

Name _____

 9 DAILY CUMULATIVE REVIEW

Write the answer.

1. 245
    − 116

2. 50
    − 28

3. 702
    + 555

4. 79
    + 52

5. 90
    − 54

6. 443
    + 149

Write the number.

7. three hundred ninety-two _____

8. three hundred two _____

9. three hundred ninety _____

10. nine hundred three _____

11. ninety-three _____

12. two hundred thirty-nine _____

Solve. Use each of the digits 2, 7, 4, and 1.

13. What is the greatest number you can write?

_____

14. What is the least number you can write?

_____

Name _____

 10 **DAILY CUMULATIVE REVIEW**

Write the answer.

1.	490 + 207	**2.**	898 − 570

3. 406
+ 33

4.   119
− 96

5. 6351
+ 2236

6. 4344
− 2203

Write each number in short word form.

7. 7,367   _____

8. 52,049   _____

9. 40,078   _____

10. 901,743   _____

11. 109,375   _____

12. 823,721   _____

Solve.

13. The gasoline automobile was invented in
1892. The parking meter was invented
43 years later. In what year was the parking
meter invented?

_____

DAILY CUMULATIVE REVIEW

Write the answer.

1. 432
  + 205

2. 631
  − 221

3. 506
  + 390

4. 8849
  − 5629

5. 5523
  + 2461

6. 7252
  − 6150

Round to the nearest ten.

7. 17 _____

8. 67 _____

9. 62 _____

10. 24 _____

11. 254 _____

12. 348 _____

13. 435 _____

14. 889 _____

15. 678 _____

16. 197 _____

Solve.

17. An apple has 80 Calories. A cup of fruit cocktail has 255 Calories. How many more Calories does a cup of fruit cocktail have than does an apple?

_____

Name _____

DAILY CUMULATIVE REVIEW

Add or subtract.

1. 33
   + 17

2. 62
   + 91

3. 96
   + 14

4. 87
   − 06

5. 25
   − 18

6. 30
   − 14

7. 53
   + 29

8. 75
   − 43

Write the numbers in order from least to greatest.

9. 451, 154, 145, 541 _____

10. 46, 4006, 406, 4106 _____

11. 1008, 108, 1018, 1081 _____

12. 8040, 8400, 4008, 4080 _____

13. 6420, 6320, 6432, 6342 _____

14. 32, 3020, 302, 320 _____

Solve.

15. Florida has 580 miles of coastline. Maine has 228 miles of coastline. How many more miles of coastline does Florida have than does Maine?

_____

13 DAILY CUMULATIVE REVIEW

Write the answer.

1. $\begin{array}{r} 37 \\ -\ 10 \\ \hline \end{array}$

2. $\begin{array}{r} 87 \\ +\ 12 \\ \hline \end{array}$

3. $\begin{array}{r} 294 \\ -\ 150 \\ \hline \end{array}$

4. $\begin{array}{r} 92 \\ +\ 74 \\ \hline \end{array}$

5. $\begin{array}{r} 84 \\ -\ 69 \\ \hline \end{array}$

6. $\begin{array}{r} 173 \\ +\ \ 29 \\ \hline \end{array}$

Write in word form.

7. 6.25 _____

8. 100.03 _____

9. 95.4 _____

10. 0.51 _____

11. 82.07 _____

12. 60.6 _____

Solve.

13. The Apollo-Saturn 10 space flight lasted 192 hours, 3 minutes, and 23 seconds. The Apollo-Saturn 11 space flight lasted 195 hours, 18 minutes, and 35 seconds. How much longer was the Apollo-Saturn 11 space flight?

_____

14 DAILY CUMULATIVE REVIEW

Add or subtract. Use mental math.

1. 90 + 50 _____   **2.** 800 − 400 _____

3. 1200 + 300 _____   **4.** 500 + 300 _____

5. 290 − 50 _____   **6.** 2000 + 1500 _____

7. 670 − 40 _____   **8.** 850 − 425 _____

Find the digit in the greatest place. Write the value of that digit in short word form.

9. 90,705   **10.** 50,690,263

_____   _____

11. 168,878   **12.** 7,009,296,000

_____   _____

Solve.

13. The record weight for an Atlantic blue marlin fish is 1282 pounds. The record weight for a Pacific blue marlin is 1376 pounds. Which fish was heavier and by how much?

_____

Name _____

Write the answer.

1.	857 + 462	**2.**	391 + 160	**3.**	5905 − 2690

4.	1209 − 185	**5.**	994 − 258	**6.**	6592 + 6336

Write the value of the underlined digit in standard form.

7. 702

8. 379

9. 2492

_____   _____   _____

10. 451,675

11. 1958

12. 673

_____   _____   _____

Solve.

13. A number is between 35 and 45. The sum of the digits is 8. If you subtract the tens digit from the ones digit, the difference is 0. What is the number?   _____

14. A number is between 150 and 200. The sum of the digits is 12. If you subtract the ones digit from the tens digit, the difference is 5. What is the number?   _____

16 ▸ DAILY CUMULATIVE REVIEW

Estimate by rounding to the greatest place.

1. $4.8 - 1.2$ _____

2. $\$36.50 + \$19.36$ _____

3. $8190 - 7428$ _____

4. $3.4 + 6.1 + 2.2$ _____

5. $237 + 169 + 794$ _____

6. $\$5.32 + \$7.02 + \$4.59$ _____

Round to the nearest hundred.

7. 334 _____   8. 268 _____

9. 4602 _____   10. 1323 _____

11. 7603 _____   12. 4589 _____

Solve.

13. From 1957 to 1988 there were 2976 successful space launches. Of these, 875 were made by the United States. How many successful launches were made by other countries?

_____

17 DAILY CUMULATIVE REVIEW

Write the answer.

1. 7499
   + 6656

2. 5066
   − 2928

3. 19,326
   − 7,541

4. 8552
     2089
   + 3268

5. $37.78
   − 28.67

6. 11,213
     5,028
   +   873

7. 4091
     7209
   + 3164

8. 9007
   − 3568

9. 10,000
   − 6,789

Write the sum. Use mental math.

10. 19 + 21 _____

11. 22 + 58 _____

12. 55 + 36 _____

13. 47 + 31 _____

Solve.

14. In 1988 the population of Phoenix, Arizona was 923,750. In the same year the population of Dallas, Texas was 987,360. Which city had the greater population? How much greater was it?

_____

Name _____

Write the answer.

1.	4.14	2.	5937	3.	7.409
	+ 7.21		− 3250		− 5.2

4.	4.2	5.	$60.18	6.	5.393
	4.3		− 39.76		2.7
	+ 8.7				+ 7.205

Compare. Write < or >.

7. 117 ◯ 107   **8.** 56 ◯ 65

9. 99 ◯ 101   **10.** 308 ◯ 803

11. 1429 ◯ 1294   **12.** 7823 ◯ 8723

13. 2 ◯ 2.01   **14.** 14.8 ◯ 14.08

Solve.

15. Mrs. Rogers plans to buy the following ingredients for potato salad: 5 pounds of potatoes for $0.99; a jar of mayonnaise for $1.39; a jar of pickles for $1.89; and celery for $0.59. To the nearest dollar, how much money should she take to the store?

_____

19 DAILY CUMULATIVE REVIEW

Write the answer.

1. 724 + 442	**2.** 6087 − 5785	**3.** 35,863 − 24,305

4. $32.45 + 17.96	**5.** 51,697 + 17,201	**6.** 301,781 − 296,238

Write the number in standard form.

7. 137 thousand

_____

8. 17 million, 6 thousand, 98

_____

9. 475 billion

_____

10. 29 billion, 8 thousand, 14

_____

Solve.

11. Attendance at the first football game of the season was 23,292. Attendance at the first basketball game was 14,935. Were there more people at the football game or at the basketball game? How many more were there?

_____

Name _____

Write the answer.

1. 200
   + 900

2. 1800
   − 300

3. 710
   + 50

4. 3000
   + 6500

5. 6000
   − 2000

6. 2900
   − 400

Compare. Write < or >.

7. 892 ◯ 895

8. 3.05 ◯ 3.5

9. 137.6 ◯ 13.76

10. 0.002 ◯ 0.025

11. 1.00 ◯ 0.99

12. 2.46 ◯ 2.406

13. 0.896 ◯ 0.899

14. 25.6 ◯ 26.5

Solve.

15. Alicia has $2.50. If popcorn costs $1.50 and orange juice costs $0.85, does Alicia have enough money to buy both items?

_____

21 ▶ DAILY CUMULATIVE REVIEW

Write the answer.

1. 3.80
     + 6.65

2. 21.78 g
     + 10.35 g

3. 9.035
     + 2.100

4. 5.09
     − 3.35

5. $13.61
     − 9.08

6. 1.779
     − 0.046

Round each number to the greatest place.

7. 871 _____

8. 1976 _____

9. 185 _____

10. 70.92 _____

11. 913 _____

12. 993 _____

13. 11.75 _____

14. $27.42 _____

Solve.

15. In 1988, Atlanta had a population of 420,000; San Jose had a population of 738,420; and St. Louis had a population of 403,700. Write the cities in order from greatest to least population.

_____

Name _____

22 DAILY CUMULATIVE REVIEW
....

Write your estimate. Remember to adjust.

1.   152
      647
  + 84

2.   28
   474
+ 544

3.   2.04
  7.16
+ 0.96

4.   3227
   582
   605
+ 4892

5. $66.23
   3.62
 13.37
+ 2.97

6.   3.39
  0.73
  6.61
+ 8.43

Write the word name for each decimal.

7. 1.01   _____

8. 0.65   _____

9. 7.016 _____

10. 60.008 _____

Solve.

11. Bob keeps a record of how far he goes each time he jogs. Last week his record showed 3.2 kilometers, 2.5 kilometers, 6.1 kilometers, and 1.5 kilometers. How far did he jog last week in all?

_____

23 ▶ DAILY CUMULATIVE REVIEW

Write the difference. Use mental math.

1. 87 cm
    − 19 cm

2. 94
    − 59

3. $9.00
    − 4.99

4. 1985
    − 999

5. $2.21
    − 0.99

6. 407 mL
    − 199 mL

Order from least to greatest.

7. 725, 752, 727, 757

8. 2.23, 3.3, 3.23, 2.32

_____

_____

9. 2963, 2936, 2966, 2693

10. 0.089, 0.809, 0.098, 8.08

_____

_____

Solve.

11. At the 1896 Olympics Thomas Burke ran the
    400-meter run in 54.2 seconds. At the 1988
    Olympics Steven Lewis ran the 400-meter
    run in 43.87 seconds. By how much was
    Steven Lewis faster than Thomas Burke?

_____

Name _____

24 DAILY CUMULATIVE REVIEW

Write the answer.

1.	67.92	2.	40.80 kg	3.	$28.71
	− 19.89		+ 25.71 kg		+ 10.98

4.	15.97	5.	5.186	6.	92.727
	− 0.931		− 3.07		+ 81.443

Round each decimal to the nearest whole number.

7. 2.96   8. $78.29   9. 13.9

_____   _____   _____

10. 62.53   11. 4.078   12. $652.26

_____   _____   _____

13. 154.52   14. 820.9   15. 49.999

_____   _____   _____

Solve.

16. As it orbits the earth, the moon's closest
    distance to the earth is 221,463 miles. The
    farthest distance is 252,710 miles. What is
    the difference between the closest and
    farthest distances?

    _____

Name _____

Write the answer.

1.　1 ft 9 in.
　　+ 8 ft 2 in.

2.　　8809
　　+ 6170

3.　$201.86
　−　39.74

4.　29,178
　− 17,581

5.　$126.44
　+　 32.66

6.　　8 min 41 s
　+ 13 min 16 s

Write the value of each expression.

7. What is n + 3 if n = 8? If n = 13?　　_____

8. What is t − 16 if t = 26? If t = 50?　　_____

9. What is 25 − r if r = 14? If r = 8?　　_____

Write an expression to describe each situation.

10. One loaf of bread can make 10 sandwiches. If b stands for the number of loaves of bread that were used, how many sandwiches were made?　　_____

11. There are 12 inches in one foot. If c feet of ribbon are needed to trim an apron, how many inches are needed?　　_____

26 ⏵ DAILY CUMULATIVE REVIEW

Write the answer.

1.   23.14
     − 19.49
     _____

2. $59.26
     + 16.32
     _____

3.   148.68
     − 50.30
     _____

4.   2.191
     + 4.54
     _____

5.   906.3
     − 42.6
     _____

6.   127.3 cm
     + 78.1 cm
     _____

Estimate. Write < or >.

7. $199 + 681 \bigcirc 900$

8. $31 + 277 + 610 \bigcirc 850$

9. $\$7.31 + \$4.06 + \$8.84 \bigcirc \$19.00$

10. $4.18 + 5.45 + 3.78 \bigcirc 12$

11. $15.6 + 28.9 + 43.7 \bigcirc 90$

Solve.

12. Mt. McKinley in Alaska is 20,320 feet tall. Round this height to the nearest hundred.

         _____

13. Mt. Whitney in California is 14,494 feet tall. How much taller is Mt. McKinley than Mt. Whitney?

         _____

Name _____

Write the answer.

1. 4187
   − 1018

2. 63,259
   + 14,969

3. 204,570
   − 142,108

4. $90.31
   86.07
   + 71.35

5. 2136
   4047
   + 7921

6. 12,031
   3,159
   + 15,854

Write the missing number. Use mental math.

7. _____ × 4 = 400

8. 50 × _____ = 250

9. 80 × _____ = 7200

10. _____ × 200 = 6000

11. 600 × _____ = 30,000

12. 25 × _____ = 1000

Solve.

13. In 1990, the Arizona-Sonora Desert Museum had a total attendance of about 600 thousand. The same year, the Cincinnati Zoo had an attendance of about 1 million, 500 thousand. About how many more people attended the Cincinnati Zoo than the Arizona-Sonora Desert Museum?

_____

28 DAILY CUMULATIVE REVIEW

Write your estimate.

1. 81
× 23

2. 47
× 12

3. 73
× 41

4. 57
× 27

5. 62
× 19

6. 59
× 35

Write the least common multiple.

7. 2, 9

8. 7, 4

_____

_____

9. 3, 4, 6

10. 2, 6, 7

_____

_____

11. 2, 5, 10

12. 3, 4, 5

_____

_____

Solve.

13. Rebecca used 4 red tiles and 10 blue tiles to decorate a wooden tray. How many tiles of each color will she need to decorate 16 trays?

_____

29 ▸ DAILY CUMULATIVE REVIEW

Write the product.

1. 124
      × 7

2. $6.45
      × 5

3. 408
      × 4

4. 529
      × 2

5. 786
      × 3

6. 461
      × 8

Write the number in short word form.

7. 62,041 _____

8. 1,507,099 _____

9. 268,007 _____

10. 16,200,158 _____

Solve.

11. Anita hikes 2.5 miles each hour. If she hikes from 9 A.M. to 1 P.M., how far will she have hiked?

_____

Name _____

30 DAILY CUMULATIVE REVIEW

Write the answer.

1.　718
　 + 884

2.　6.54
　 − 2.63

3.　38
　 × 23

4.　529
　 × 14

5.　$71.86
　 +   2.89

6.　49,091
　 − 12,263

Write the product. Use mental math.

7. 40 × 60 _____

8. 6 × 5 × 5 _____

9. 2000 × 6 _____

10. 9 × 2 × 5 _____

11. 50 × 90 _____

12. 600 × 3 _____

Solve.

13. Ryoichi is participating in a bike-a-thon. His friends have pledged to donate a total of $3.10 for each mile he rides. If Ryoichi rides for 23 miles, will he raise more or less than $60?

_____

Name _____

31 DAILY CUMULATIVE REVIEW

Write the answer.

1. 2.570
   + 0.194

2. 52.83
   − 6.49

3. 0.722
   − 0.431

4. 25.47
   + 14.82

5. 35.287
   − 8.309

6. 179.29
   + 48.91

Write the word name for each decimal.

7. 0.793 _____

8. 38.18 _____

9. 500.02 _____

Solve.

Gasoline Purchases		
Day	Amount	Cost
Monday	10.5 gallons	$13.55
Thursday	8.7 gallons	$11.22
Saturday	4.9 gallons	$6.62

10. Frieda kept a log of her gasoline purchases. How much did she spend on gasoline during the week?

11. How many gallons of gasoline did Frieda buy during the week?

_____   _____

Name _____

 32 **DAILY CUMULATIVE REVIEW**

Write the answer.

1. 357
       244
    + 607

2. 3513
       1603
    + 844

3. 4105
    − 2780

4. 63,913
    − 29,026

5. 90,448
    − 1,859

6. 138,799
    + 125,883

Order from least to greatest.

7. 5.98, 0.985, 0.598, 5.89   _____

8. 460, 406, 466, 40.6   _____

9. 65.3, 56.6, 56.3, 605.3   _____

10. 7.6, 7.69, 7.612, 7.129   _____

Solve.

11. In Fresno, California the average rainfall is 2.0 inches in January, 1.9 inches in February, and 1.6 inches in March. What is Fresno's average monthly rainfall for those months?

_____

Name _____

Write the product.

1.	102 × 5	2.	37 × 7	3.	136 × 25

4.	21 × 80	5.	268 × 117	6.	461 × 240

Complete.

7. $905 \times 7 = (900 \times \underline{\hspace{1cm}}) + (\underline{\hspace{1cm}} \times 7)$

8. $2025 \times 4 = (\underline{\hspace{1cm}} \times 4) + (25 \times \underline{\hspace{1cm}})$

9. $6 \times 75 = (6 \times \underline{\hspace{1cm}}) + (6 \times \underline{\hspace{1cm}})$

10. $160 \times 3 = (100 \times \underline{\hspace{1cm}}) + (\underline{\hspace{1cm}} \times 3)$

Solve.

11. Mrs. Hom drove at an average rate of 52 miles per hour from 1 P.M. until 5 P.M. How far did she drive?

_____

12. After stopping for supper, Mrs. Hom drove 120 more miles. Did she drive more or less than 300 miles that day?

_____

Name *Miranda* 10\2\00 *Lindsey*

$100 - 0$

34 DAILY CUMULATIVE REVIEW

Write the answer.

1.
```
  8058
+ 3904
 11962
```

2.
```
  77,299
- 17,145
  60,154
```

3.
```
    63
  ×  7
   443
```

4.
```
  35,443
-  4,610
  30,633
```

5.
```
    385
  ×  99
   3425
 +34650
  38115
```

6.
```
  269,522
+  13,008
  282,530
```

Round each number to the greatest place.

7. 8.62   9.00

8. $58.45 $60.00

9. 6523   7000

10. 61,526   60,000

11. $24.89 $20.00

12. 765   800

Solve.

13. In 1989, there were 202,027 births in the New England states and 291,145 births in New York state. Round each number to the nearest ten thousand.

200,000 births 290,000 births

14. About how many births in all were there in New York and the New England states in 1989?

493,172

```
  202,027
+ 291,145
  493,172
```

Name _____

Write your estimate.

1. 49 × 21

2. 6840 + 5941

_____

_____

3. 774 × 3

4. 30,321 − 4728

_____

_____

5. 148 × 37

6. 4280 − 635

_____

_____

Write the number in standard form.

7. 2 million, 701 thousand, 99 _____

8. 5 billion, 6 million, 12 _____

Solve.

9. Jane Austen was an English writer who lived from 1775 to 1817. Robert Burns was a Scottish poet who lived from 1759 to 1796. How many years did each writer live?

_____

10. How many years after the birth of Robert Burns was Jane Austen born?

_____

Add or subtract. Use mental math.

1. 500 + 600 _____   2. 490 − 100 _____

3. 8000 − 600 _____   4. 31 + 68 _____

5. 65 cm + 28 cm _____   6. 600 + 900 + 150 _____

Write the value of each expression.

7. What is $t - 10$ if $t = 17$? If $t = 50$? _____

8. What is $31 + s$ if $s = 9$? If $s = 12$? _____

9. What is $r + 12$ if $r = 13$? If $r = 26$? _____

10. What is $45 - n$ if $n = 19$? If $n = 39$? _____

11. What is $j - 83$ if $j = 95$? If $j = 150$? _____

12. What is $28 + p$ if $p = 17$? If $p = 42$? _____

Solve.

13. Felicia wants to give each of her 2 cousins a
gift of a CD. If CDs cost $11.99 each and the
sales tax on each is $0.48, can Felicia buy
the two gifts for $25?

_____

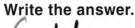

Name _Miranda_ 10/2/00

Write the answer.

1. 8.946
   + 5.126
   ‾‾‾‾‾‾
   14.072

2. 79.5⁴⁰
   − 2.433
   ‾‾‾‾‾‾
   77.107

3. 201
   × 3
   ‾‾‾‾
   603

4. 79
   × 17
   ‾‾‾‾
   '553
   +790
   ‾‾‾‾
   1343

5. $1.52
   × 47
   ‾‾‾‾‾
   $10.64
   +60.80
   ‾‾‾‾‾
   $71.44

6. 143.07
   − 43.81
   ‾‾‾‾‾
   99.26

Write the least common multiple.

7. 5, 6, 15   _30_

8. 4, 7, 12   _84_

9. 10, 15, 20   _20_

10. 5, 8, 16   _80_

11. 3, 5, 9   _45_

12. 2, 6, 7   _42_

13. 5, 10, 15   _30_

14. 2, 6, 8   _24_

Solve the problem. Making notes may help you.

15. Susan charges $1.50 per hour to baby-sit for
1 child, and $2.25 per hour for 2 children. On
Saturday, Susan baby-sat for 1 child from
1 P.M. to 3 P.M. and then baby-sat for
2 children from 4 P.M. to 6 P.M. How much did
she earn in all?

_$9.00_

Name _____

Write the answer.

1.   29,000
       + 18,863
       _47,863_

2.   8.351
       − 0.653
       _7.698_

3. $75.93
       + 31.14
       _$107.07_

4.   338,647
       − 155,832
       _183,215_

5.   4.063
       + 7.093
       _11.156_

6.   179.49
       −   3.07
       _176.42_

Complete. Write >, <, or =.

7. 7 × 12 ⟩ 10 × 8
      84   80

8. 9 × 60 = 18 × 30
      540   540

9. 6 × 43 < 4 × 92
      258   368

10. 46 × 25 > 35 × 21

11. 27 × 54 = 18 × 81
      1458   1458

12. 19 × 7 < 8 × 26

Solve.

13. To the nearest hundred
miles, estimate the
distance from Bangkok
to each city.

Bejing 2000
_____

Chicago 8600
_____

London 5900
Montreal 8300

Air Distances from Bangkok to Other Cities	
City	Miles
Bejing	2046
Chicago	8570
London	5944
Montreal	8338

14. What is the round-trip distance
from Bangkok to London?

4888 miles
5944

Name _____

Write the answer.

1. 6457
+ 7461
14918

2. 807
× 12
819

3. 9)216
24
− 18
36
− 36
0

4. 309 56856
× 184
1236
24720
+30900
56856

5. 73.78
− 7.92
65.86

6. 7)497
71
− 49
07
− 7
0

Write the missing number.

7. 35 ÷ 5 = 7

8. 60 ÷ 6 = 10

9. 1 ÷ 8 = 8

10. 27 ÷ 3 = 9

Solve.

11. Ruth earned $40 last week by washing windows for her mother. Ruth worked for 8 hours. How much did she earn per hour?

$5 _____

12. Ruth plans to earn $60 next week. How long will she have to work if she is paid the same hourly wage?

12 hours _____

40 DAILY CUMULATIVE REVIEW

Write the product.

1. 58
× 18

2. 63
× 46

3. 90
× 67

4. 479
× 126

5. 570
× 384

6. 615
× 140

Write the value of the expression when $r = 2$; when $r = 6$.

7. $\frac{24}{r}$

8. $31 - r$

9. $\frac{60}{r}$

10. $78 + r$

Solve.

11. Martin bought sandwiches for himself and 3 friends. He bought 1 Cheddar cheese sandwich and 3 tuna sandwiches. How much did he pay?

$5.05

Sandwich	Price
Cheddar Cheese	$1.25
Swiss Cheese	$1.45
Tuna	$1.60
Egg Salad	$1.50
Peanut Butter	$0.95

12. Ariadni bought 2 sandwiches of the same kind for $2.90. What did she buy?

Swiss Cheese

Name _____

Write your estimate.

1. $5\overline{)391}$ 2. $3\overline{)830}$ 3. $9\overline{)4767}$

4. $6\overline{)2526}$ 5. $4\overline{)37,664}$ 6. $7\overline{)48,664}$

Compare. Write <, >, or =.

7. 8 million 13 $\bigcirc$ 409,526

8. 780,432 $\bigcirc$ 780 thousand 434

9. 5 billion 8 million $\bigcirc$ 8 billion 5 million

10. 0.426 $\bigcirc$ four hundred twenty-six thousandths

Solve.

11. By 1990, the movie *E.T.* made $228,618,939 in sales and the movie *Star Wars* made $193,500,000 in sales. Which movie made more money?

_____

12. The show *Chorus Line* played for 6,137 performances on Broadway. *Fiddler on the Roof* played for 3,242 performances on Broadway. How many more performances of *Chorus Line* were there than of *Fiddler on the Roof*?

_____

Name _____

Write the answer.

1.   9182
    3009
 + 857
   13,048

2.   169
   3581
 + 6203
  9953

3. 59,512
 + 31,955
  91,467

4.   768
 × 20
 15360

5.   318
 × 19
 2862
+3180
 6042

6.   761
 × 74
 3044
+53270
 36314

Round each number to the nearest hundred.

7. 5013   5000

8. 7473   7500

9. 4409   4400

10. 2567   2600

11. 8949   8900

12. 1275   1300

Solve the problem. Making notes may help you.

13. Library fines are $0.10 a day for children's books and $0.20 a day for adult books. Cass has 4 children's books and 2 adult books that are 7 days overdue. How much is her fine?

    80¢

43 ◤ DAILY CUMULATIVE REVIEW

Write the quotient. Use mental math.

1. 60 ÷ 30 _____   **2.** 250 ÷ 50 _____

3. 4900 ÷ 7 _____   **4.** 1000 ÷ 20 _____

5. 16,000 ÷ 8 _____   **6.** 360 ÷ 40 _____

Write the number in standard form.

7. five and six tenths _____

8. thirty-seven and two hundredths _____

9. seven hundred ninety-two thousandths _____

10. five and fifty-four thousandths _____

Solve.

11. Mrs. Brown and her two daughters are planning a train trip. Mrs. Brown's ticket will cost $84 and tickets for her daughters will cost $59 each. About how much will the train tickets cost?

_____

12. Mrs. Brown plans to spend no more than $35 a day for food for herself and her daughters while traveling. If they travel for 6 days, is $200 enough to cover the food costs? Why or why not?

_____

Name _____

••

Find the answer.

1. 85,599
  − 23,986

2. 20,229
  + 14,521

3. 713,506
  − 309,175

4. 301
  × 141

5. 841
  × 298

6. 744
  × 364

Write the value of each expression.

7. What is $c + 3$ if $c = 20$? If $c = 47$?   _____

8. What is $h - 9$ if $h = 30$? If $h = 17$?   _____

9. What is $36 - s$ if $s = 12$? If $s = 9$?   _____

10. What is $16 + p$ if $p = 15$? If $p = 34$?   _____

Solve the problem. Making notes may help you.

11. Philip spent 6 hours making 3 wooden towel
racks. The cost of materials was $3 and he
sold each rack for $12. How much money did
Philip make? How much money did he make
per hour less his expenses?

_____

Name _____

Write the quotient.

1. 5)32

2. 7)91

3. 12)64

4. 52)804

5. 75)892

6. 38)594

7. 26)475

8. 43)478

9. 64)807

Give the total cost. Use mental math.

10. 3 pounds of
    peaches at $0.99
    per pound

11. 2 loaves of banana
    bread at
    $1.99 a loaf

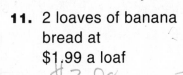

12. 5 jars of peanut
    butter at $1.99 a jar

13. 3 pens that cost
    $0.49 each

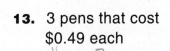

14. 6 pencils at
    $0.19 apiece

15. 7 folders at
    $0.99 apiece

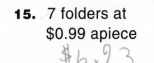

46 DAILY CUMULATIVE REVIEW

Write the answer.

1. 2.366
    + 2.902

2. 3.66
    − 1.872

3. 500
    × 16

4. 21)8590

5. $11.65
   16.02
   + 27.19

6. 40)3370

Write an expression to describe each situation.

7. Justin has 24 marbles. His brother
   gives him more marbles. If *m*
   stands for the number of marbles
   his brother gives him, how many
   marbles does Justin have?   _____

8. There are 16 ounces in a pound.
   If *p* stands for the number of
   pounds of sunflower seeds in a
   bag, how many ounces are in the
   bag?   _____

9. Arthur had $75 in his savings
   account. If *n* stands for the
   number of dollars he withdrew,
   how much does he have left in his
   account?   _____

Name _____

Write the answer.

1. 7885
    + 5903
    13,788

2. 9813
    − 6798
    3015

3. 26,703
    + 15,046
    41,749

4. 32,012
    − 6,297
    25,115

5. 709,065
    + 33,545
    742,610

6. 878,650
    − 255,083
    623,567

7. 704,729
    + 140,027
    844,756

8. 603,034
    − 296,845
    307,189

9. 849,302
    + 95,642
    944,944

Round each number to the greatest place.

10. 86.7 _*900*_

11. $22.85 _*$30.00*_

12. 611 _*600*_

13. 6582 _*7000*_

14. 378.3 _*4000*_

15. 4.6 _*5.0*_

Solve.

16. The average annual snowfall in Anchorage,
    Alaska, is 85.8 inches. In Erie, Pennsylvania
    the average annual snowfall is 68.5 inches
    of snow. How much more snow does
    Anchorage usually get than Erie?

    _*17.3*_

48 ▶ DAILY CUMULATIVE REVIEW

Write the answer.

1. 85
   × 17

2. 344
   × 142

3. 540
   × 96

4. 8)403

5. 32)624

6. 51)624

Write the number in expanded form.

7. 807 _____

8. 94,040 _____

9. 7,000,132 _____

10. 28,400 _____

11. 5,907,027 _____

Solve.

12. United States water usage averages
168 gallons of water per person per day.
About how much water is used per person
in a year?

_____

Name _____

Write the answer.

1.   3.82
    + 9.21

2.   0.858
    − 0.031

3.   93,019
    + 7,023

4. $80.15
      11.40
    + 52.76

5.   76.279
    − 3.109

6.   6152
       819
    + 2514

Write the value of each expression.

7. What is $m + 11$ if $m = 9$? If $m = 24$? _____

8. What is $27 + v$ if $v = 10$? If $v = 27$? _____

9. What is $39 - t$ if $t = 18$? If $t = 5$? _____

10. What is $r - 4$ if $r = 23$? If $r = 41$? _____

Solve.

11. In 1988 there were 108,720 registered
cocker spaniels in the United States. In 1989
the number had risen to 111,636. How many
more cocker spaniels were there in 1989
than in 1988?

_____

Name _____

Write the answer.

1. 9)75   **2.** 62   **3.** 4534
                × 31   − 330

4. 16)203   **5.** 63.4 km   **6.** 186
               + 4.2 km   × 502

Write the least common multiple.

7. 3, 8 _____   **8.** 2, 9 _____

9. 3, 12 _____   **10.** 3, 10, 12 _____

11. 2, 5, 7 _____   **12.** 2, 3, 7 _____

Solve.

13. Bristlecone pines are thought to be the oldest
living trees in the world. Some are estimated to
be about 4600 years old. The oldest known
redwood trees are about 3500 years old. About
how much older than the oldest redwoods are
the oldest bristle cone pines?

_____

Name _____

Estimate by rounding to the greatest place.

1. 6.2 + 3.9   **2.** 9.305 – 0.623   **3.** $20.40 – $6.33

_____   _____   _____

4. 12,066 + 4055 **5.** 1761 – 872   **6.** $168.84 + $79.55

_____   _____   _____

Write the greatest common factor.

7. 8, 15 _____   **8.** 6, 9 _____

9. 4, 22 _____   **10.** 16, 24 _____

11. 30, 40 _____   **12.** 17, 22 _____

Solve.

13. Melinda is selling tickets to the
school play. Tickets cost $3.50 for
adults, $2.00 for students, and
$1.50 for members of the drama
club. So far, Melinda has sold 16
adult tickets, 10 student tickets,
and 5 tickets to drama club
members. How much money has
she collected?   _____

52 DAILY CUMULATIVE REVIEW

Write the answer. Use mental math.

1. 75 + 16 _____

2. 70 × 50 _____

3. 49 m + 23 m _____

4. 180 − 99 _____

5. $9.20 − $2.99 _____

6. 300 × 40 _____

7. 750 − 115 _____

8. 52 × 3 _____

9. 698 − 350 _____

10. $1.49 + $ 3.49 _____

Write the prime factorization for each number.

11. 33 _11X3_
11 x 3

12. 24 _2X2X2X3_
4X6
2X2X3 7X7

13. 50 _5 X2X5_
10X5

14. 49 _7X7_
7X7

15. 27 _3X3X3_
3X9
3X3X3

16. 42 _3X2X7_
6X7
2X2X3

Solve.

17. An apple pie has 2920 Calories. If the pie is divided into 8 equal slices, how many Calories are there in each slice?

365 calories per piece

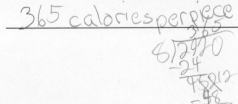

Name _____

Write your estimate.

1. 63×3 _____

2. 88×69 _____

3. 133×9 _____

4. 121×7 _____

5. 49×24 _____

6. 67×31 _____

7. 28×43 _____

8. 62×36 _____

Copy each number sentence. Then use parentheses to make the sentence true.

9. $90 \div 10 + 5 = 6$ $90 \div (10 + 5) = 6$

10. $8 + 3 \times 9 = 99$ $(8 + 3) \times 9 = 99$

11. $6 \times 3 + 2 \div 2 = 15$ $6 \times (3 + 2) \div 2 = 15$

12. $49 \div 1 + 6 + 2 = 9$ $49 \div (1 + 6) + 2 = 9$

13. $20 \times 4 + 25 \div 5 = 85$ $(20 \times 4) + 25 \div 5$

14. $8 \times 7 + 9 \div 2 = 64$ $8 \times (7 + 9) \div 2 = 64$

Solve.

15. Mr. Chadda bought a set of
16 mugs for his office for $96.
How much did each mug cost? _____

Name _____

Write the answer.

1. 16)211

2. 7)98

3. 9)290

4. 81)748

5. 46)700

6. 41)552

Estimate the quotient.

7. 5)242

8. 7)1689

9. 962 ÷ 6

_40~50_ ____280~290____ ____160~170____

10. 3563 ÷ 4 **11.** 19,624 ÷ 6 **12.** 6563 ÷ 8

__1000~1010__ ___330~340___ ___870~880___

Solve.

13. Mitra, Shapar, and Maryam
are cousins. Their heights are
48 inches, 52 inches, and
53 inches. What is their
mean height? _____

Name _____

Write the answer.

1. 4.18
   + 7.62

2. 68,971
   − 5,685

3. 59
   × 34

4. 56⟌298

5. 185
   × 6

6. 135,809
   − 37,476

Write the answer. Write whether you used a calculator or mental math.

7. 5 × 872 _____

8. 14 + 32 _____

9. 8000 ÷ 100 _____

10. 7700 − 695 _____

11. 7835 × 92 _____

12. 66,519 ÷ 19 _____

Solve.

13. A children's magazine has a circulation of 345,011. A teen magazine has a circulation of 593,790. What is the combined circulation of the two magazines?

_____

Name _____

Write the answer.

1. 111
     × 21
     111
   +2220
    2331

2. 5)435
      87
     -40
      35
     -35
       0

3. 26)878

4. 627
     × 268

5. 400
     × 342

6. 16)311

Write *prime* or *composite* for each number.

7. 82 _____   **8.** 29 _____

9. 51 _____   **10.** 41 _____

Solve.

11. Robert kept track of the time he spent watching television during the school week. What was the median, mean, and range of his television watching?

Day	TV Time
Monday	3 hours
Tuesday	4 hours
Wednesday	1 hours
Thursday	2 hours
Friday	5 hours

_____

Name _____

Write the answer.

1. 80.05 + 9.51	**2.** 7118 − 820	**3.** 30,248 − 18,995

4. $8.39 6.82 + 6.93	**5.** 3862 3097 + 6277	**6.** 5005 4540 + 920

Round each number to the nearest hundred.

7. 1050 _____   **8.** 910 _____

9. 1850 _____   **10.** $8425 _____

Solve.

Snack	Price
Salad	$2.25
Milk	$0.55
Fruit Cup	$1.50
Sandwich	$2.75
Juice	$0.75

11. Rajan has $3.00 to spend at the snack bar.
What can he buy?

_____

58 DAILY CUMULATIVE REVIEW

Write the product. Use mental math.

1. 1000×7 _____   **2.** 90×50 _____

3. 200×30 _____   **4.** 700×60 _____

5. 80×40 _____   **6.** 2000×6 _____

7. $5 \times 3 \times 4$ _____   **8.** $8 \times 5 \times 6$ _____

Write an expression to describe each situation.

9. Alice needs 2 feet of fabric for each apron she makes. If *a* stands for the number of aprons she makes, how much fabric does she need?

_____

10. Mrs. Rodriguez made 36 rolls for a dinner party. If *r* stands for the number of rolls that were eaten, how many rolls were left over?

_____

11. Jeffrey had 25 rubber stamps. For his birthday he received a set of cartoon character rubber stamps. If *c* stands for the number of new stamps he received, how many rubber stamps does he have in all?

_____

Name _____

Write the answer.

1. $5\overline{)485}$ 2. $9\overline{)158}$ 3. $8\overline{)308}$

4. $6\overline{)628}$ 5. $4\overline{)461}$ 6. $7\overline{)936}$

Write the range and the mean for each. You may use a calculator.

7. 37, 56, 64, 30, 48   _____

8. 4, 13, 8, 11, 19, 17   _____

9. $189, $163, $146, $225, $182   _____

Solve the problem.

10. The Desert Hills School is planning a field trip to the aquarium. There will be 275 people góing, and each bus can seat 66 people.

   a. How many buses are needed?   _____

   b. How many empty seats will there be?_____

   c. If the same number of people ride each bus, how many people will be on each bus?

   _____   _____

Name _____

60 DAILY CUMULATIVE REVIEW

Write the answer.

1. 174
    × 5

2. 46
    × 17

3. 33
    × 22

4. 24)156

5. 39)719

6. 16)591

Write the equivalent measure. You may use the Table of Measures in your math book.

7. A piece of rope is 72 inches long. How many feet is this?

_____

8. A bag of rice weighs 80 ounces. How many pounds is this?

_____

9. A movie lasts for 120 minutes. How many hours is this?

_____

10. The track for a race is 600 yards long. How many feet is this?

_____

Solve.

11. It costs $239 to rent an economy car for 1 week. At this rate, about how much is paid per day to rent the car?

_____

61 ► DAILY CUMULATIVE REVIEW

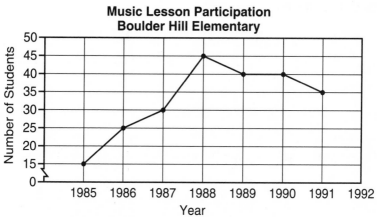

**Music Lesson Participation
Boulder Hill Elementary**

Use the graph to answer each question.

1. The after-school music program began in 1985. How many students participated in the program the first year? _____

2. In what year did the greatest number of students participate in the program? How many students participated that year? _____

3. Write *a*, *b*, or *c* . The graph shows that since 1988 the number of students participating has generally
  a. been increasing.
  b. remained the same.
  c. been decreasing. _____

4. In what years did 40 students participate? _____

Name _____

 DAILY CUMULATIVE REVIEW

Write the answer.

1. 865
    589
    + 376

2. 7301
    − 2282

3. 4829
    268
    + 5093

4. 355
    − 67

5. 15,108
    + 6,256

6. 190,143
    − 89,100

Write the value of the expression when $r = 5$; when $r = 10$.

7. $\frac{20}{r}$ _____

8. $\frac{r}{5}$ _____

9. $15 + r$ _____

10. $\frac{60}{r}$ _____

11. $r \cdot 7$ _____

12. $23 - r$ _____

Solve.

13. Melissa is packing snacks for a camping trip. She plans on bringing 3 snacks for each person. How many snacks does she need to pack for 32 people? _____

DAILY CUMULATIVE REVIEW

Write the answer.

1. 707.1
        95.3
      + 344.4

2.   156
        × 152

3. 6) 592

4.   95
       × 71

5.   2779
       − 1406

6. 26) 798

Write the first three common multiples.

7. 6, 8

8. 4, 16

9. 2, 4, 9

_____   _____   _____

Solve.

10. A box of strawberries costs $0.89. A box of raspberries costs $1.59. How much more than 5 boxes of strawberries do 5 boxes of raspberries cost?

11. A flat of 12 boxes of strawberries costs $7.92. What is the price per box of strawberries purchased by the flat?

_____   _____

Name _____

Write the quotient.

1. $5\overline{)500}$ **2.** $30\overline{)270}$ **3.** $7\overline{)21,000}$

4. $6\overline{)3000}$ **5.** $90\overline{)7200}$ **6.** $50\overline{)40,000}$

Write the missing digit.

7. 8.23 is between 8 and 9 but is closer to _____ .

8. $5.98 is between $ _____ and $ _____ but is closer to $ _____ .

9. 7.3 is rounded to _____ .

10. 749 is rounded to _____ hundred.

Solve.

11. In 1990, the governor of California received a salary of $102,079. The same year, the governor of Kentucky received a salary of $69,730. How much more did the governor of California receive than did the governor of Kentucky?

_____

Name _____

Write your estimate.

1. $\begin{array}{r} 48 \\ \times\ 3 \\ \hline \end{array}$

2. $34\overline{)604}$

3. $\begin{array}{r} 57 \\ \times\ 11 \\ \hline \end{array}$

4. $\begin{array}{r} 695 \\ \times\ 4 \\ \hline \end{array}$

5. $19\overline{)3810}$

6. $27\overline{)85,087}$

Write an exercise that has each of the following answers. Use at least two operations.

7. 3 _____

8. 5 _____

9. 10 _____

10. 15 _____

11. 16 _____

12. 19 _____

13. 60 _____

14. 100 _____

Solve.

15. Because of fog, an airplane flight scheduled to depart at 6:00 A.M. did not take off until 7:45 A.M. How long was the flight departure delayed?

_____

66 DAILY CUMULATIVE REVIEW

Write the answer.

1. $7.10
    × 6

2. 305
    × 9

3. 582
    × 29

4. 261
    × 48

5. 47 cm
    × 5

6. 329
    × 73

Use the set of figures to answer each question. There is one large and one small size of each figure.

7. Which figures are either circles or are small?

_____

8. Which figures are either large or are triangles?

_____

9. Which figures are not square or rectangles?

_____

10. Which quadrilaterals are not small?

_____

Name _____

67 DAILY CUMULATIVE REVIEW

....

Write the answer.

1. $76\overline{)423}$ **2.** $80\overline{)905}$ **3.** $17\overline{)386}$

4. $68\overline{)473}$ **5.** $22\overline{)260}$ **6.** $54\overline{)401}$

Write the greatest common factor for each set of numbers.

7. 9, 27 _____ **8.** 30, 45 _____

9. 24, 32 _____ **10.** 10, 12, 20 _____

Solve each problem. If there is not enough information, tell what you need to know.

11. Junior has some dollar bills, a quarter, some dimes, and a nickel. Does he have enough money to buy a magazine that costs $2.50? Explain.

_____

_____

12. Mrs. Shapiro's car travels 25 miles per gallon of gas. If the car has 10 gallons of gas in the tank, is there enough gas to drive to Chicago?

_____

_____

Name _____

Write the answer. Use mental math.

1. 19×5 _____   2. $700 + 300$ _____

3. $\$1.99 \times 6$ _____   4. $\$0.49 \times 5$ _____

5. $60 + 90 + 40$ _____   6. $100 + 700 + 800$ _____

Order the numbers from least to greatest.

7. 173, 110, 210, 117 _____

8. 1.35, 1.53, 1.03, 1.15 _____

9. 32.8, 28.3, 30.2, 28.8 _____

10. 4010, 4001, 4012, 4011 _____

Solve.

11. Mrs. Watson bought 160 yards of fabric for costumes for the drama club. If each costume requires 3 yards of fabric, how many costumes can be made?

_____

12. At the autumn carnival, the student council made $143 selling food and $85 selling tickets. How much did they make in all?

_____

Name _____

Use the graph below.

Acts for the Lincoln School Spring Show

4 Comedy Acts

2 Magic Acts

8 Singing Acts

4 Dance Acts

6 Acrobatic Acts

1. How many acts in all were in the Lincoln School Spring Show?

_____

2. How many singing acts were in the Lincoln School Spring Show?

_____

3. What fraction of the acts were magic acts?

_____

4. What fraction of the acts were acrobatic acts?

_____

5. How many singing, comedy, and dance acts were there in all?

_____

6. All the singing and dancing acts went on before intermission. What fraction of the show was complete at intermission?

_____

Name _____

Write the answer.

1.   0.260
  + 0.092

2.   1.97
  − 1.81

3.   83.60
  − 25.06

4.   10.006
  + 4.809

5.   0.711
  − 0.300

6.   56.09
  − 3.83

Complete. Write >, <, or = .

7. 9×16 ◯ 4×20

8. 3×30 ◯ 6×15

9. 8×10 ◯ 5×20

10. 7×40 ◯ 8×30

11. 6×80 ◯ 7×70

12. 7×11 ◯ 15×5

13. 3×27 ◯ 9×9

14. 4×14 ◯ 6×11

Solve.

15. The Kirpalani family went on a camper vacation for 2 weeks. They traveled an average of 175 miles per day. How many miles did they travel in all?

_____

16. The camper averaged 35 miles per gallon of gas and the family spent $77.70 on gas. What was the average price paid per gallon of gas?

_____

Name _____

Estimate by rounding to the greatest place.

1. $11.41 - 3.2$ _____ **2.** $64.1 - 39.5$ _____

3. $4173 - 2859$ _____ **4.** $82 + 57 + 99$ _____

5. $7.8 + 3.6 + 0.8$ _____ **6.** $6.25 + 1.75 + 5.95$ _____

Write the prime factorization. Use a factor tree.

7. 54 _____ **8.** 70 _____

9. 49 _____ **10.** 75 _____

Solve the problem. Use estimation.
Explain how you got your answer.

11. Last year, the library bought 192 new books.
If the library buys about the same number of
books each year, about how many books will
they buy in the next 3 years?

_____

DAILY CUMULATIVE REVIEW

Write the answer.

1.
```
  42
  50
+ 17
```

2.
```
  473
×   9
```

3. $60\overline{)548}$

4.
```
  0.101
- 0.072
```

5. $37\overline{)602}$

6.
```
  57
× 28
```

Write the value of each expression.

7. What is $t + 6$ if $t = 9$? If $t = 12$? _____

8. What is $27 - s$ if $s = 7$? If $s = 21$? _____

9. What is $p - 4$ if $p = 8$? If $p = 20$? _____

10. What is $x + \frac{1}{2}$ if $x = 8$? If $x = 14$? _____

Solve.

11. Can Sara and 3 friends divide 52 cards evenly?

_____

12. If 144 photos are divided equally into 4 photo albums, how many will be in each album?

_____

Name _____

Write the product. Use mental math.

1. 70 × 80 _____

2. 1000 × 6 _____

3. 90 × 500 _____

4. 5 × 700 m _____

5. 80 yd × 60 _____

6. 90 × 900 _____

7. 5 × 3 × 8 _____

8. 9 × 2 × 5 _____

Complete. Use the Table of Measures in your math book.

9. 192 in. = _____ ft

10. 420 min = _____ h

11. 816 oz = _____ lb

12. 61 yd = _____ ft

Solve.

13. How many 5-pound bags of flour can be made from 730 ounces of flour?

_____

14. How many 3-pound bags of apples can be made from 1250 pounds of apples?

_____

15. How many 2-yard tablecloths can be made from 150 feet of fabric?

_____

16. How many 24-inch hair ribbons can be made from 10 yards of ribbon?

_____

Name _____

Write the answer.

1.	12.2	2.	0.317	3.	4.743
	− 8.91		− 0.15		+ 5.079

4.	$94.04	5.	67.21	6.	16.098
	+ 83.32		− 17.8		+ 4.982

Write an equivalent decimal.

7. 4.10 _____

8. 0.01 _____

9. 12.52 _____

10. 678.80 _____

11. 3.45 _____

12. 0.7 _____

Solve the problem. Work backward or use other strategies.

13. Meena plans to have a party on December 12. A week before the party, she has to let the caterer know exactly how many people will be coming. She wants to mail the invitations 10 days before she must give the information to the caterer. When should she mail the invitations?

_____

Name _____

Use the graph to answer each question below.

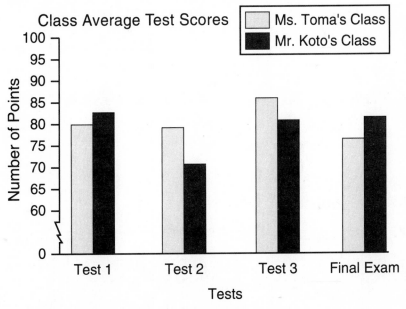

1. Which class did better on Test 1? _____

2. On which test was the average score for Ms. Toma's class more than 85 points? _____

3. On which test did the two classes have the largest difference in their average scores? _____

4. Which class did better on the final exam? _____

5. Which class scored a better average test score for the entire course? _____

Name _____

76 DAILY CUMULATIVE REVIEW

Write your estimate. Remember to adjust.

1. 294 + 991

2. 5732 − 2577

3. 4.3 + 9.8 + 2.6

4. 9.5 + 5.41 + 6.73

5. 1276 − 632

6. $13.44 − $6.25

7. 9.54 − 1.17

8. 579 + 497 + 115

9. 17.65 + 9.42

10. 348 + 685

Measure the width of each button to the nearest $\frac{1}{4}$ inch.

11.

12.

13.

Name _____

77 DAILY CUMULATIVE REVIEW

Write the answer.

1. 61,706
    + 20,868

2. 7137
    − 1679

3. 262
    ×   6

4. 8)184

5. $9.73
    ×   18

6. 48)15,840

Copy each number sentence. Then use parentheses to make the sentence true.

7. $9 \div 2 + 1 + 5 = 8$ _____

8. $8 + 6 \times 6 + 1 = 50$ _____

9. $30 \div 6 + 4 = 3$ _____

10. $81 \div 3 \times 3 = 9$ _____

11. $8 - 2 \times 7 = 42$ _____

Solve. Use the map on page 180 in your math book if you need help.

12. Maureen lives in Portland, Oregon. At 7:45 A.M. she called a friend in Washington, D.C. What time was it in Washington, D.C.? _____

78 DAILY CUMULATIVE REVIEW

Write the answer.

1. 9 h 20 min
   + 3 h 35 min

2. 8 h 39 min
   − 5 h 33 min

3. 49 h 28 min
   + 17 h 12 min

4. 30 min 24 s
   − 19 min 6 s

5. 5 min 13 s
   + 6 min 7 s

6. 47 min 25 s
   − 24 min 1 s

7. 14 h 15 min
   − 7 h 45 min

8. 12 min 28 s
   − 5 min 39 s

9. 26 min 44 s
   + 18 min 27 s

Write the missing number. Use mental math.

10. _____ · 3 = 300

11. 20 · _____ = 1000

12. _____ · 300 = 1500

13. 90 · _____ = 6300

14. 6 · _____ = 2400

15. _____ · 200 = 1800

Solve.

16. Arturo has an herb garden in his
    backyard. The herb garden is in
    the shape of a hexagon. How
    many sides does Arturo's herb
    garden have? _____

Name _____

Write your estimate.

1. $7\overline{)1018}$ **2.** $80\overline{)658}$ **3.** $6\overline{)9657}$

4. $77\overline{)5034}$ **5.** $8\overline{)25,309}$ **6.** $49\overline{)26,554}$

Write the perimeter of each polygon.

7.
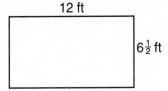
12 ft

$6\frac{1}{2}$ ft

_____

8.
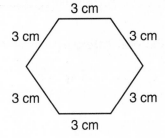
3 cm

3 cm   3 cm

3 cm   3 cm

3 cm

_____

9.
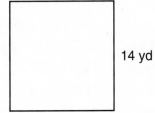
14 yd

_____

10.
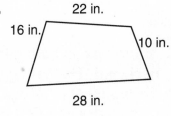
22 in.

16 in.   10 in.

28 in.

_____

Name _____

 80 DAILY CUMULATIVE REVIEW

Write the answer.

1. $6\overline{)95}$ **2.** $\begin{array}{r} 77 \\ \times\ 59 \\ \hline \end{array}$ **3.** $\begin{array}{r} \$55.97 \\ +\ 29.75 \\ \hline \end{array}$

4. $\begin{array}{r} 154 \text{ mi} \\ -\ 22 \text{ mi} \\ \hline \end{array}$ **5.** $3\overline{)76}$ **6.** $\begin{array}{r} 65 \\ \times\ 83 \\ \hline \end{array}$

Write each product. Make a model if you need to.

7. 5 × 7 tenths _____   **8.** 4 × 5 tenths _____

  5 × 0.7 _____   4 × 0.5 _____

9. 8 × 4 tenths _____   **10.** 3 × 3 tenths _____

  8 × 0.4 _____   3 × 0.3 _____

Solve.

11. The mean weight of 4 dogs in a pet show was 22 pounds. The weights of 3 of the dogs were 18 pounds, 27 pounds, and 10 pounds. How much did the fourth dog weigh?

_____

Name _____

Write the quotient. Use mental math.

1. $20\overline{)4000}$ **2.** $9\overline{)900}$ **3.** $30\overline{)2700}$

4. $6\overline{)18,000}$ **5.** $90\overline{)810}$ **6.** $8\overline{)6400}$

Write the median, mean, and range.

7. 61 in., 52 in., 59 in., 68 in., 55 in.

_____

8. $185, $280, $273, $160, $197, $231

_____

9. 22°, 15°, 19°, 5°, 14°, 33°

_____

Solve. Use estimation.

10. Lamar has $15 to spend on school
supplies. He wants to buy 2 notebooks
at $1.49 each, a dictionary for $6.95,
and a set of markers for $5.95. Does he
have enough money?   _____

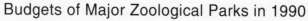

Budgets of Major Zoological Parks in 1990

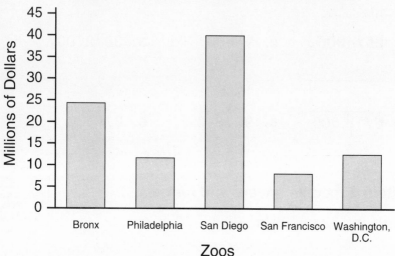

Zoos

Use the graph to write the answer. Use estimation.

1. Which zoos had a budget greater than $20 million?

_____

2. About how much was the budget for the
Washington, D.C. Zoo?

_____

3. Which zoo had a budget of less than $10 million?

_____

4. About how much greater than the Philadelphia
Zoo's budget was the Bronx Zoo's budget?

_____

Name _____

Write the answer. Write whether you used a calculator or mental math.

1. 1835 + 100

2. 649 × 15

3. 9467 − 2810

4. 80 ÷ 2

5. 391 ÷ 17

6. 2 × 5 × 16

Use the map on page 180 if you need to. Write the time in Santa Fe, New Mexico, when it is:

7. 8 A.M. in Los Angeles. _____

8. 5 P.M. in Boston. _____

9. noon in Chicago. _____

10. 8:30 P.M. in Denver. _____

Solve.

11. To roast a large turkey at 325°F, allow 15 minutes cooking time for each pound of turkey. If you begin roasting a 20-pound turkey at noon, when will it be done?

_____

Write the product. Use squared paper if you need help.

1.	5.2	2.	7.1	3.	2.6
	× 3		× 4		× 7

4.	14.8	5.	27.2	6.	18.4
	× 5		× 6		× 4

Write the value of each expression.

7. What is $k + 1$ if $k = 8$? If $k = 17$? _____

8. What is $19 - w$ if $w = 2$? If $w = 12$? _____

9. What is $8 + h$ if $h = 0$? If $h = 8$? _____

10. What is $c - 5$ if $c = 30$? If $c = 45$? _____

11. What is $15 + d$ if $d = 7$? If $d = 15$? _____

12. What is $25 - n$ if $n = 8$? If $n = 0$? _____

Solve.

13. Mavis picks out 12 party favors and a tablecloth for a party. The party favors are $2.39 each. The tablecloth is $7.99. Will Mavis spend more than $35.00? _____

Name _____

Add or subtract. Use mental math.

1. 2000 + 6500 _____ **2.** $53.00 − $19.99 _____

3. 64 + 25 _____ **4.** 1070 − 800 _____

5. 74 − 29 _____ **6.** 36 ft + 49 ft _____

Write the name of each polygon. Choose the name from the box below.

pentagon	nonagon
octagon	hexagon

7.

8.

9.

_____ _____ _____

Solve.

10. In 1990, the *Anchorage Times* newspaper in Alaska had a daily circulation of 32,777 newspapers. The Salt Lake City *Tribune* newspaper in Utah had a daily circulation of 112,630 that same year. How much greater was the Salt Lake City *Tribune*'s circulation than the circulation of the *Anchorage Times*?

Name _____

Write the answer.

1. 9.2
    5.07
  + 4.95

2. 401.921
  − 83.075

3. $74.00
    28.18
  + 57.09

4. 486
  ×   3

5. 47)611

6. 65
  × 19

Find the digit in the greatest place. Write the value of that digit in short word form.

7. 25,600

8. 405,195

9. 4,905,793

_____   _____   _____

10. 874

11. 7,038,327

12. 31,074

_____   _____   _____

Solve the problem. Work backward or use other strategies.

13. Mr. Allyn plans to install a rectangular swimming pool that is 20 feet by 25 feet. What will be the perimeter of the swimming pool?

_____

87 DAILY CUMULATIVE REVIEW

Write the product.

1. 4.07
    ×   9

2. 0.08
    ×   3

3. 0.125
    ×   1

4. 0.68
    ×   8

5. 5.6
    × 5

6. 3.008
    ×   7

Use the drawing of the hexagon.

7. What is the greatest number of diagonals that can be drawn from one vertex?

_____

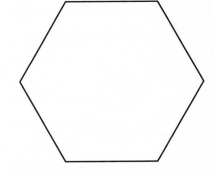

8. What is the total number of diagonals that can be drawn in the hexagon?

_____

Solve.

9. Pam checks the thermometer before leaving the house. The temperature is 85°F. Does she need to wear a jacket?

_____

88 DAILY CUMULATIVE REVIEW

Write the answer.

1. $7\overline{)97}$ 2. $8\overline{)523}$ 3. $9\overline{)954}$

4. $3\overline{)510}$ 5. $38\overline{)646}$ 6. $59\overline{)297}$

Write the letter of the more reasonable temperature.

7. a cup of hot chocolate   **a.** 105°F **b.** 50°F _____

8. the ocean on a summer day   **a.** 40°F **b.** 70°F _____

9. a glass of water with ice   **a.** 8°C **b.** 20°C _____

10. a fall day in the mountains   **a.** 13°C **b.** 33°C _____

Solve.

11. In 1988, 93,464 students were enrolled in elementary and secondary schools in Vermont. That same year, 97,793 students were enrolled in Wyoming elementary and secondary schools. Which state had more students in 1988?

_____

Name _____

Write the answer.

1. 3967
   + 3655

2. $7.39
   ×   80

3. 48,489
   − 17,559

4. 19)3387

5. 18 lb 4 oz
   + 4 lb 2 oz

6. 917
   × 186

Compare. Write <, >, or = .

7. 6931 ◯ 6931.0

8. 20.57 ◯ 20.507

9. 5.9 ◯ 4.95

10. 0.102 ◯ 0.120

11. 5.98 ◯ 9.058

12. 0.03 ◯ 0.030

13. 0.56 ◯ 6.5

14. 1.43 ◯ 1.41

Solve.

15. Shelled walnuts cost $3.69 per pound. Cream cheese costs $1.90 per pound. How much does it cost to buy 2.5 pounds of walnuts and 1.5 pounds of cream cheese?

_____

90 DAILY CUMULATIVE REVIEW

Write your estimate.

1. $4\overline{)948}$ **2.** $29\overline{)650}$ **3.** $72\overline{)4064}$

4. $1824 \div 26$ **5.** $867 \div 6$

_____   _____

6. $3251 \div 56$ **7.** $8044 \div 81$

_____   _____

Complete.

8. 5.09 m = _____ cm   **9.** 60 mm = _____ m

10. 26 m = _____ km   **11.** 59 cm = _____ mm

12. 750 cm = _____ m   **13.** 1.5 km = _____ m

Solve.

14. Mr. Hom wants to install tiles in his workshop. The room's floor measures 3 meters by 2.5 meters. He can buy tiles that are 0.15 m along a side or 0.25 m along a side. Which size tile will fit exactly along both the length and the width of his workroom? How many tiles does he need in all?

_____

91 DAILY CUMULATIVE REVIEW

Write the product. Round dollar amounts to the nearest cent.

1. $7.42
 × 1.25

2. 7.8
 × 3.3

3. $0.66
 ×   0.5

4. 3.78
 × 0.1

5. $9.08
 ×   100

6. 0.51
 × 8.9

Write *prime* or *composite* for each number. If a number is composite, give its prime factorization.

7. 17 _____

8. 52 _____

9. 61 _____

10. 85 _____

Solve.

11. Geraldo has a bookcase that is 1.5 meters wide. He wants to put it on a wall that is 160 centimeters wide. Is the wall wide enough for the bookcase?

_____

Write the answer.

1. 3.03
    × 6

2. 12)‾3296‾

3. 99.534
    + 0.000

4. 9.559 kg
    − 1.457 kg

5. 1.03
    × 0.9

6. 6)‾4212‾

Solve each problem. Write whether you estimated or computed the exact answer.

7. Is $20 enough to buy the sweater and the canvas shoes?

_____

Item	Cost
Sweater	$15.95
Activity Book	$ 3.95
Canvas Shoes	$ 7.00
Board Game	$ 9.95

8. Melinda paid for 3 activity books with a 20-dollar bill. How much change did she receive?

_____

9. Does the sweater cost more or less than the canvas shoes and the board game together?

_____

93 DAILY CUMULATIVE REVIEW

Write the product. Use mental math.

1. 7.54×10

2. 0.55×100

_____

_____

3. 1.901×1000

4. 187.5×100

_____

_____

5. 0.09×10

6. 9.24×1000

_____

_____

Choose the numbers that are compatible. Write *a*, *b*, or *c*.

7. $8\overline{)205}$ **a.** $8\overline{)160}$ **b.** $8\overline{)200}$ **c.** $8\overline{)210}$ _____

8. $4\overline{)922}$ **a.** $4\overline{)900}$ **b.** $4\overline{)800}$ **c.** $4\overline{)1000}$ _____

9. $7\overline{)335}$ **a.** $7\overline{)330}$ **b.** $7\overline{)300}$ **c.** $7\overline{)350}$ _____

Solve.

10. Ms. Alvarez has a square flower bed that measures 6 feet on each side. She wants to put a plant in each corner and at 2-foot intervals around the edge. How many plants does she need in all? _____

Name _____

Write the product.

1. 6.01	2. 0.96	3. 0.03
× 4	× 3	× 6
24.04	2.88	0.18

4. 17.5	5. 4.25	6. 8.28
× 4	× 26	× 73
70		

Write how much time will pass.

7. from 2:30 P.M. to 5:45 P.M. _____ 3 hours 15 min.

8. from 6:00 A.M. to 2:30 P.M. _____ 8 hours 30 min.

9. from 4:20 P.M. to 9:49 P.M. _____ 5 hours 29 min.

10. from 10 P.M. to 3:15 A.M. _____ 5 hours 15 min.

Solve.

11. Marianna works in a flower shop. Her boss gave her a large bunch of cut flowers to use in bouquets and centerpieces. She used 6 flowers in a centerpiece. With half of the remaining flowers she made 3 bouquets of 10 flowers each and had 1 flower left over. How many flowers did she start with?

_____ 37

95 DAILY CUMULATIVE REVIEW

Write the answer.

1.
$$1825$$
$$235$$
$$+\ 940$$

2.
$$158$$
$$\times\ 49$$

3. $18\overline{)490}$
$$-36$$
$$130$$
(handwritten: 2 above, answer work)

4.
$$59{,}585$$
$$-\ 15{,}958$$

5.
$$2\text{ lb }3\text{ oz}$$
$$+\ 1\text{ lb }8\text{ oz}$$

6.
$$\$2.43$$
$$\times\qquad 3$$

Round each number to the greatest place.

7. 285 _____

8. $1047 _____

9. 73.24 _____

10. 33,790 _____

11. 6502 _____

12. 4.62 _____

Solve.

13. Quick Record mini-cassette recorders are packed 12 in a carton for shipping. If the company shipped 150 cartons of mini-cassette recorders in a week, how many tape recorders did they ship?

_____

96 DAILY CUMULATIVE REVIEW

Write your estimate.

1. $637 + 527$

2. $9028 - 3669$

_____

3. $3316 + 1897$

4. $2244 - 617$

_____

5. $82,805 - 13,272$

6. $\$45.33 + \$27.10$

_____

7. $59 + 601 + 47 + 410$

8. $3.7 + 9.85 + 8.12 + 4.38$

_____

Write the equivalent measure. Use the Table of Measures in your math book.

9. A box of building blocks weighs 960 ounces. How many pounds is this?

10. On Saturday, the library is open for 240 minutes. How many hours is this?

_____

11. Miranda is 48 inches tall. How many feet is this?

12. A redwood tree is 33 yards tall. How many feet is this?

_____

Name _____

 DAILY CUMULATIVE REVIEW

Tell what compatible numbers you would use, then estimate the quotient.

1. $7\overline{)\$266}$ _____ **2.** $9\overline{)\$50.73}$ _____

3. $2\overline{)\$8.57}$ _____ **4.** $8\overline{)\$94.63}$ _____

5. $6\overline{)\$104.22}$ _____ **6.** $4\overline{)\$14.57}$ _____

Write the perimeter.

7. Square: side = 14 ft _____

8. Regular hexagon: side = 49 cm _____

9. Rectangle: length = 6 yd, width = 2 yd _____

10. Regular triangle: side = 3.7 cm _____

Solve.

11. Leticia practiced the piano from 3:20 P.M. until 4:10 P.M. Billy practiced from 4:15 P.M. until 5:00 P.M. Who practiced longer? How much longer?

_____

Write the product. Round dollar amounts to the nearest cent.

1. $5.89
   × 3.9

2. 345
   × 0.03

3. 7.6
   × 0.6

4. 5.17 × 100 _____

5. $0.17 × 4.4 _____

6. 366.8 × 1.8 _____

7. 1.4 × $1.95 _____

8. $62.03 × 2.5 _____

9. 1.01 × 1.01 _____

Estimate.

10. Can you buy 2 pen
    and pencil sets with
    $10?

    _____

Item	Cost
Pen and Pencil Set	$5.49
School Binder	$3.29
Mechanical Pencil	$1.74
Stapler	$8.98

11. Can you buy 3 school binders
    with $10?   _____

12. Can you buy 10 mechanical
    pencils with $20?   _____

13. Can you buy 6 staplers with $50?   _____

14. About how much would it cost
    altogether if you bought one of
    each item on the list?   _____

99 ▸ DAILY CUMULATIVE REVIEW

Write the answer.

1. 40 min 17 s − 8 min 6 s	**2.** 16 min 10 s + 37 min 40 s	**3.** 15 min 22 s + 5 min 26 s

4. 41 h 50 min
  − 19 h 1 min
	5. 35 h 9 min
	  − 28 h 7 min
		6. 14 h 8 min
		  + 5 h 51 min

Estimate. Write < or >.

7. 2509 + 367 ◯ 2700

8. 245 + 89 + 351 ◯ 900

9. $2.14 + $61.01 ◯ $65.00

10. 91 + 821 + 471 ◯ 1200

Solve.

11. Elizabeth I was the queen of England from 1558 to 1603. For how many years was she queen? _____

12. The Wars of the Roses were fought in England from 1455 to 1485. For how many years did these wars last? _____

100 DAILY CUMULATIVE REVIEW

Write the quotient.

1. $6\overline{)33}$ -30 ~~5~~

2. $2\overline{)13}$ -12 $\overline{0}$ 6 r 5

3. $5\overline{)\$28}$ -25 $\$5$ 60

4. $18 \div 8$ _2 r 2_

5. $51 \div 6$ _8 r 3_

6. $\$25 \div 4$ _\$6.10_

7. $35 \div 8$ _4 r 3_

Write the answer.

8. $6 \div 6 + 10$ _11_

9. $13 - 3 + 1 \times 5$ _55_

10. $8 \times 3 + 2$ _26_

11. $4 + 0 \times (5 + 2)$ _22_

Solve the problem. Making notes may help you.

12. Duane earns $5 an hour at a canning factory. For every hour he works over 20 hours a week, he earns an extra $1.50 per hour. One week he worked 20 hours and on Saturday he worked from 9:00 A.M. to 3 P.M. How much did he earn that week?

_\$100_

Name _____

Write the answer.

1.   4.367
      − 2.978

2. 9)56.7

3.   20.602
      + 17.373

4.   1.82
      × 0.8

5. $707.14
      −   86.47

6. 2)4.802

Write the least common multiple.

7. 2, 8, 7

8. 2, 4, 12

9. 6, 10, 15

_____ _____ _____

Solve.

10. Esperanza, Leola, and Bonnie sing together as a trio. For their performances, they want to make similar dresses, each in a different color. The fabric they chose comes in peach, yellow, and lime. Bonnie and Esperanza do not want to wear lime. What choices do they have of who wears which color?

_____

_____

Name _____

Number of Books Read by 5th and 6th Grade Classes

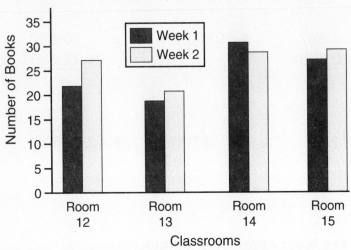

Use the graph to answer each question.

1. In which rooms did the students read more than 20 books in week 1?

   _____

2. In which room did the students read the most books during the 2 weeks?   _____

3. In which room was the difference in the number of books read between week 1 and week 2 the greatest?   _____

4. In which room did the students read the fewest books during the 2 weeks?   _____

103 DAILY CUMULATIVE REVIEW

Write the answer. Use your mental math rules.

1. 4.99×10 _____ **2.** $96.2 \div 100$ _____

3. 0.62×100 _____ **4.** $5.1 \div 1000$ _____

5. $0.02 \div 10$ _____ **6.** 4.79×1000 _____

7. $5.1 \div 10$ _____ **8.** 76.92×100 _____

Write the word name for each decimal.

9. 5.68 _____

10. 19.001 _____

11. 2000.074 _____

12. 43.71 _____

13. 305.04 _____

Solve.

14. May bought a ticket to the circus for
$6.50, a package of peanuts for $1.25,
and a souvenir program for $2.25.
How much did she have left from $10? _____

Name _____

104 DAILY CUMULATIVE REVIEW

Write your estimate.

1. 6 × 353 _____ **2.** 18 × 61 _____

3. 2014 ÷ 7 _____ **4.** 690 ÷ 27 _____

5. 79 × 47 _____ **6.** 73,754 ÷ 88 _____

Complete.

7. 403 × 6 = (400 × _____) + (_____ × 6)

8. 9 × 270 = (9 × _____) + (_____ × 70)

9. 3 × 88 = (3 × _____) + (3 × _____)

10. 708 × 2 = (700 × _____) + (8 × _____)

11. 83 × 9 = (80 × _____) + (3 × _____)

12. 7 × 605 = (7 × _____) + (7 × _____)

Solve.

13. Maurice is selling souvenir hats at the Mid-Summer Parade. He bought the hats for $2 each and sells them for $4 each. How many hats must he sell to make a profit of $100? _____

Copyright © Houghton Mifflin Company. All rights reserved.

Name _____

 DAILY CUMULATIVE REVIEW

Write the quotient. Estimate or think about a related multiplication sentence to place the decimal point.

1. 6)‾0.618   **2.** 9)‾20.7   **3.** 5)‾10.15

4. 0.036 ÷ 4 _____   **5.** $48.12 ÷ 6 _____

6. 3.12 ÷ 3 _____   **7.** 21.014 ÷ 7 _____

Complete.

8. 98,643 m = _____ km   **9.** 31 cm = _____ mm

10. 0.13 m = _____ mm   **11.** 62 mm = _____ m

12. 689 cm = _____ m   **13.** 5.35 km = _____ m

Solve.

14. Ruth paid $12.50 for a set of 10 glasses. How much did each glass cost?

_____

15. Hal spent $7.00 on 100 lead sinkers for his fishing tackle box. How much did each lead sinker cost?

_____

106 DAILY CUMULATIVE REVIEW

Write the answer.

1. $9.51
    ×   10

2. 83)‾3086

3.   9.06 cm
      7.92 cm
    + 4.39 cm

4.   13.4 kg
    − 6.5 kg

5.   37 mi
    × 11

6. 4)‾$5

△**DEF** is the slide image of △**ABC**.
Complete each statement.

7. △ ABC ≅ _____

8. ∠ BCA ≅ _____

9. $\overline{AC}$ ‖ _____

10. $\overline{AB}$ ≅ _____

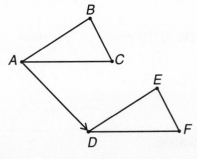

Solve. You may use a calculator.

11. Last season Maria had the best
    batting average on her team. She
    had 28 hits and was at bat 64 times.
    What was her batting average?   _____

Name _____

Write the product. Use mental math.

1. 6.93×10 _____ **2.** 0.264×100 _____

3. 0.006×1000 _____ **4.** 9.082×10 _____

5. 15.4×100 _____ **6.** 40.91×1000 _____

7. 0.104×10 _____ **8.** 9.16×100 _____

Write the letter of each triangle that is:

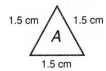
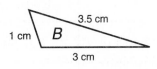

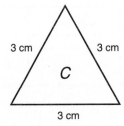
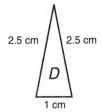

9. equilateral _____

10. isosceles _____

11. scalene _____

Name _____

Write your estimate.

1. 316 – 78 _____   **2.** 9042 + 4820 _____

3. 39 × 27 _____   **4.** 30,654 ÷ 7 _____

5. 9 × 536 _____   **6.** 2.4 + 3.8 + 1.4 _____

Complete. What time is it in the other 3 cities?

	Boston	Dallas	Tucson	Sacramento
	9 A.M.	8 A.M.	7 A.M.	6 A.M.
7.	7:20 P.M.			
8.		2:19 P.M.		
9.			5:40 A.M.	
10.				1:00 A.M.

Solve.

11. Bill bought 4 bags of potatoes at a
farm stand. The bags weighed
5.9 pounds, 6.2 pounds, 4.1 pounds,
and 7.8 pounds. He needs
20 pounds of potatoes to make
potato salad for a party. Does he
have enough?   _____

Name _____

Write the answer.

1. $7.60
    × ____4

2. 5)‾3‾4‾4‾

3. 64)‾2‾1‾3‾

4. $4760.67
      563.78
    +   74.19

5.   5432
    − 1889

6.   83
    × 47

Compare. Write <, >, or =.

7. 8023 ◯ 8122

8. 40.2 ◯ 42.0

9. 0.67 ◯ 0.067

10. 6.5 ◯ 6.50

11. 13.61 ◯ 16.13

12. 4806 ◯ 4086

Solve. If there is not enough information, tell what you need to know.

13. The manager of the Princeton Hills movie theater allows at least 15 minutes between showings of a film. If the first showing is at 12:30 P.M., what is the earliest time that the next showing could begin?

_____

Name _____

Write the answer. Round dollar amounts to the nearest cent.

1.
$$
\begin{array}{r}
\$8.27 \\
\times\ 1.6 \\
\hline
4962 \\
8270 \\
\hline
\$13.23
\end{array}
$$

2.
$$
\begin{array}{r}
3.86 \\
\times\ 2.2 \\
\hline
772 \\
7720 \\
\hline
8.492
\end{array}
$$

3.
$$
\begin{array}{r}
\$0.43 \\
\times\ 0.8 \\
\hline
\$0.344
\end{array}
$$

4. 3) 19.2

5. 4) 91

6. 6) $51 $8.50

Write the median, mean, and range.

7. 40 lb, 58 lb, 46 lb, 71 lb, 65 lb

56 median

8. $393, $578, $388, $528, $758, $661

_____

9. 39 yr, 3 yr, 37 yr, 71 yr, 69 yr, 9 yr

_____

Solve.

10. Percy followed the directions for a treasure hunt. He started facing north, then turned a half-turn to the right, and then a three-quarter turn to the left. What direction did he wind up facing?   west

Name _____

Write the answer. Use your mental math rules.

1. 7.18 ÷ 10 _____   **2.** 537 ÷ 10 _____

3. 0.6 ÷ 100 _____   **4.** 9.08 ÷ 100 _____

5. 27.6 ÷ 1000 _____   **6.** 880 ÷ 1000 _____

7. 9.4 ÷ 100 _____   **8.** 627.9 ÷ 1000 _____

Write *yes* or *no*.

9. Is Figure *A*
   a. a square?   _____

   b. a rectangle?   _____

   c. a parallelogram?   _____

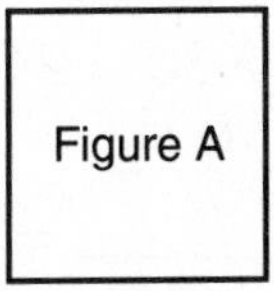

Figure A

10. Is Figure *B*
   a. a square?   _____

   b. a rhombus?   _____

   c. a parallelogram?   _____

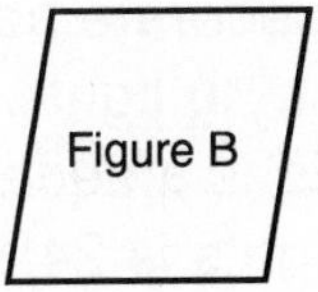

Figure B

11. Is Figure *C*
   a. a square?   _____

   b. a trapezoid?   _____

   c. a parallelogram?   _____

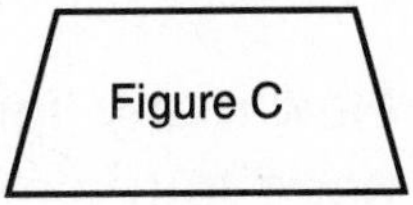

Figure C

Name _____

 DAILY CUMULATIVE REVIEW

Write the answer.

1. 25.084
 + 17.238

2. 950,599
 − 198,003

3. 4.3
 ×   9

4. 9 lb 6 oz
 + 7 lb 4 oz

5. 5)‾9‾

6. 5.17
 × 8.5

Write the missing number. Use mental math.

7. _____ · 30 = 2400   **8.** 100 · _____ = 7000

9. 9000 · _____ = 18,000   **10.** _____ · 500 = 40,000

Solve. Use one of the strategies you have learned.

11. To decorate her house for a party, Bianca wants
to string lights around the edge of her patio. Her
patio is a square, 17 feet on a side. Each string
of lights is 24 feet long and has 12 light bulbs
spaced 2 feet apart.

a. How many strings of lights does
Bianca need?   _____

b. How many light bulbs will she
need to remove so there is no
overlap?   _____

Name _____

Write the answer.

1. $28\overline{)5488}$ **2.** $70\overline{)5151}$ **3.** $62\overline{)17,050}$

4. $\begin{array}{r} 565 \\ \times\ 268 \end{array}$ **5.** $\begin{array}{r} 381 \\ \times\ 369 \end{array}$ **6.** $\begin{array}{r} 117 \\ \times\ 280 \end{array}$

Write the answer. Write whether you used a calculator or mental math.

7. $28 + 42$ **8.** $16,535 - 8496$

_____ _____

9. $98 \times 43 \times 0$ **10.** $1008 \div 18$

_____ _____

11. Trevor bought 10 goldfish for $0.49 each. How much did he spend in all? _____

12. Teresa wants to buy 2 hamsters for $6.10 each, a hamster cage for $24.35, and a bag of hamster food for $3.29. What will the total cost be? _____

Name _____

Write your estimate.

1. $4.95 + $8.19

2. 8221 − 766

_____

_____

3. 71 × 4

4. 5476 ÷ 8

_____

_____

5. $66.58 − $38.43

6. 3958 ÷ 29

_____

_____

7. 26 × 58

8. 3596 + 1246

_____

_____

Find the perimeter.

9.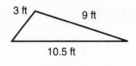

3 ft   9 ft

10.5 ft

10.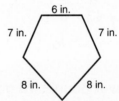

6 in.

7 in.   7 in.

8 in.   8 in.

_____

_____

11.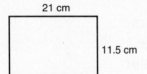

21 cm

11.5 cm

12.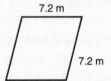

7.2 m

7.2 m

_____

_____

Write the answer. Use mental math.

1. 380 + 200

2. 915 − 200

3. 58 ft + 37 ft

4. $4.29 − $1.99

5. 86 + 24

6. 200 − 99

About how much does 1 of each of the following cost?

7. 5 avocados for $2.39 _____

8. 12 oranges for $1.00 _____

9. 4 baskets for $22.50 _____

Solve.

10. Last week Billie Jo ran 3 laps in 6.3 minutes. What was her average time for each lap? _____

11. This week her average time for 3 laps was 5.9 minutes. By how much did she improve her total time for the 3 laps? _____

Name _____

Write the answer.

1. $2\overline{)13.4}$

2. 922
× 7

3. $58.56
− 3.99

4. 23.57 cm
9.62 cm
+ 12.63 cm

5. $9\overline{)674}$

6. 0.59
× 0.8

Write the word form and the standard form of the fraction that tells what part is shaded.

7.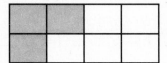

_____

8.

_____

9.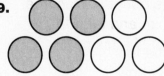

_____

10.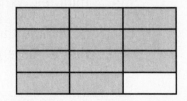

_____

117 DAILY CUMULATIVE REVIEW

Write the product. Use mental math.

1. 90×50 _____ **2.** 300×70 _____

3. 5×39 _____ **4.** $3 \times \$1.99$ _____

5. $6 \times \$0.49$ _____ **6.** 4×99 _____

7. $4 \times 6 \times 5$ _____ **8.** $8 \times 5 \times 5$ _____

Write the missing angle measure for each triangle.

9. $\triangle ABC$ $\angle A = 20°$ $\angle B = 70°$ $\angle C =$ _____

10. $\triangle LMN$ $\angle L = 79°$ $\angle M = 30°$ $\angle N =$ _____

11. $\triangle RST$ $\angle R = 95°$ $\angle S = 15°$ $\angle T =$ _____

Solve.

12. Yehuda plans to make a box from a sheet of paper that is 8 inches wide and 10 inches long. He will cut $1\frac{1}{2}$-inch squares out of each corner. Then he will fold the flaps up and tape them. What will the dimensions of his box be?

_____

Name _____

118 DAILY CUMULATIVE REVIEW

....

Tell what compatible numbers you would use, then estimate the quotient.

1. $7)\overline{\$2.59}$ _____ **2.** $6)\overline{\$53.75}$ _____

3. $5)\overline{\$0.67}$ _____ **4.** $7)\overline{\$435.19}$ _____

5. $9)\overline{\$6.63}$ _____ **6.** $8)\overline{91.80}$ _____

Identify the polygons as regular or irregular. Write *regular* or *irregular*. If a polygon is irregular tell why.

7. _____

_____

8. _____

_____

9. _____

_____

10.  _____

_____

Name _____

Write the answer.

1.
```
  2 1
  1861
  4601
+ 1571
  8033
```

2.
```
  7 9 1 1
  1.801 kg
- 0.038 kg
  1.763 kg
```

3.
```
  $2.83
×   100
  $0.00
  $00.00
× $283.00
  $28300
```

4.
```
       3.09
  4)12.36
   -12
     03
      0
     36
    -36
      0
```

5.
```
  68.3
+  1.1
  69.4
```

6.
```
   674
×  298
  5392
 60660
+134800
 200852
```

Complete to make equivalent fractions.

7. $\frac{1}{2} = \frac{6}{12}$

8. $\frac{4}{5} = \frac{8}{10}$

9. $\frac{4}{10} = \frac{2}{5}$

10. $\frac{3}{6} = \frac{1}{2}$

11. $\frac{6}{8} = \frac{3}{4}$

12. $\frac{4}{6} = \frac{2}{3}$

13. $\frac{7}{21} = \frac{1}{3}$

14. $\frac{10}{25} = \frac{2}{5}$

15. $\frac{35}{40} = \frac{7}{8}$

Solve.

16. Luella divided her flower garden into equal areas for growing marigolds, daisies, and snap dragons. What fraction of her garden is planted in marigolds?

 ⅓ _____

120 DAILY CUMULATIVE REVIEW

Write the answer.

1. 468.074
    270.123
    + 59.934
    798.13¹

2. 93.002
    − 13.126
    79.876

3. 7.9
    × 0.8
    6.32

4. 4)2.424 .606
    −24
    02
    −0
    24
    −24

5. 2)9 4.5
    −8
    10
    −10

6. 1.9
    × 3
    5.7

Write an equivalent fraction that is in simplest form.

7. $\frac{10}{12}$ _5/6_

8. $\frac{4}{20}$ _1/5_

9. $\frac{6}{36}$ _1/6_

10. $\frac{12}{16}$ _3/4_

11. $\frac{12}{24}$ _1/2_

12. $\frac{3}{15}$ _1/5_

13. $\frac{22}{33}$ _2/3_

14. $\frac{7}{21}$ _1/3_

15. $\frac{60}{75}$ _4/5_

16. $\frac{15}{40}$ _3/8_

17. $\frac{32}{48}$ _2/3_

18. $\frac{6}{8}$ _3/4_

Solve.

19. Four friends participated in a walk-a-thon to raise money for a local charity. Feliz raised $9.35, Paula raised $14.17, Alfonso raised $6.70, and Kingsley raised $7.56. Did they raise an average of $10 each? _____

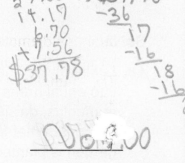

Name _____

 DAILY CUMULATIVE REVIEW

Write your estimate.

1. 9.7 – 5.97 _____   **2.** 7.08 + 3.7 _____

3. 17 × 67 _____   **4.** 676 ÷ 31 _____

5. 749 + 87 _____   **6.** 9877 – 8143 _____

7. 5 × 29 _____   **8.** 38,691 ÷ 8 _____

Order the numbers from least to greatest.

9. 601, 611, 160, 161 _____

10. 4.57, 5.47, 4.75, 5.74 _____

11. 9652, 9419, 9625, 9941 _____

Solve. Use mental math.

12. The diameter of the planet Pluto is about 3600 miles. The diameter of Earth is about 7900 miles. How much greater than the diameter of Venus is Earth's diameter? _____

13. Jupiter's diameter is almost 21 times the diameter of Mars. The diameter of Mars is about 4200 miles. About how many miles is the diameter of Jupiter? _____

Name _____

 DAILY CUMULATIVE REVIEW

Write the answer.

1. $7.78
× 6

2. 42.002
× 6

3. 1.31
× 0.7

4. 4$\overline{)11}$

5. 3$\overline{)12.48}$

6. 5$\overline{)0.355}$

Complete. Write >, <, or =.

7. 84 cm $\bigcirc$ 1.4 m

8. 13 m $\bigcirc$ 0.013 km

9. 2505 mm $\bigcirc$ 2.5 m

10. 72 mm $\bigcirc$ 8 cm

11. 1600 cm $\bigcirc$ 1.6 km

12. 0.007 km $\bigcirc$ 700 cm

Solve.

13. A jogging path at Sunrise Park is $1\frac{1}{3}$ miles long. The jogging track at the high school is $1\frac{1}{4}$ miles long. Would 10 times around the Sunrise Park jogging path be a longer or shorter distance than 10 times around the high school jogging track?

_____

DAILY CUMULATIVE REVIEW

Use the graph to answer each question.

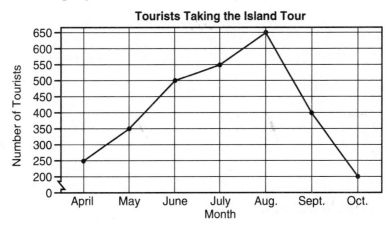

Tourists Taking the Island Tour

1. In which month did the most tourists take the Island Tour?

   August

2. Between which two months did the number of tourists increase the most? Decrease the most?

   May and June, and August and Sept

3. In which months did at least 400 tourists take the Island Tour?

   June, July, Aug, Sept.

4. Write a, b, or c. ___C___
   The graph shows that after August the number of tourists generally
   a. increases. **b.** remains the same. **c.** decreases.

DAILY CUMULATIVE REVIEW

Write the answer.

1.
$$0.9\overline{)2.7}$$
3
-27
0

2.
$$5\overline{)287}$$
57 r2
-25
37
-35
2

3.
69,579
$- 32,112$
37,467

4.
22
356
$\times\ 14$
1424
$+3560$
4984

5.
9.6
$\times\ 3$
28.8

6.
1
4.01 kg
2.7   kg
$+\ 1.683$ kg
8.393 Kg

Write each number in standard form.

7. 53 million _____ 53,000,000

8. 3 million, 56 thousand _____ 3,056,000

9. 40,000 + 5000 + 40 + 9 _____ 45,049

Write each fraction as a decimal.

10. $\frac{16}{50}$ .32

11. $\frac{7}{8}$ .875

12. $\frac{3}{8}$ .375

13. $\frac{20}{64}$ .3125

14. $\frac{100}{40}$ 2.5

15. $\frac{17}{4}$ 4.25

Solve.

16. Order the fractions in exercises 10–15 from least to greatest.

$\frac{20}{64}, \frac{16}{50}, \frac{3}{8}, \frac{7}{8}, \frac{100}{40}, \frac{17}{4}$

Name _____

Write the answer. Use mental math.

1. $21 + $69 = _____   **2.** 610 − 500 = _____

3. 6.8 × 100 = _____   **4.** 450 ÷ 5 = _____

5. 1200 + 700 = _____   **6.** 4000 − 700 = _____

7. 2 × 14 × 5 = _____   **8.** 300.9 ÷ 10 = _____

Write the greatest common factor for each set of numbers.

9. 4, 12 _____   **10.** 7, 8 _____

11. 15, 25 _____   **12.** 24, 42 _____

13. 6, 12, 30 _____   **14.** 8, 24, 60 _____

15. 15, 30, 40 _____   **16.** 18, 30, 33 _____

Read the story. Does the underlined sentence make sense? Explain.

17. Craig practiced the violin for 45 minutes.
Melinda practiced the violin for $\frac{3}{4}$ of an hour.
Melinda practiced for a longer time than
Craig practiced.

_____

_____

Name _____

 126 DAILY CUMULATIVE REVIEW

Write your estimate.

1. 1739
   − 803

2. 6909
   + 7840

3. 594
   × 9

4. 5)9254

5. 9777
   − 216

6. 21.3
   + 46.9

Solve. Use the diagram. Write the answer in simplest form.

Karin's Berry Farm

	Strawberries 3 acres	
Raspberries 1 acre	Blueberries 2 acres	

7. How many acres is Karin's Farm? _____

8. What fraction of the entire farm is planted with blueberries? _____

9. What fraction of the entire farm is planted with raspberries or strawberries? _____

DAILY CUMULATIVE REVIEW

Write the answer.

1.	2.	3.
3 h 42 min	17 min 38 s	38 min 19 s
+ 1 h 5 min	− 4 min 30 s	+ 12 min 19 s

Use figure *LMNP* and its grid to answer each question.

4. Write the ordered pair that names

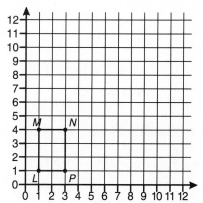

   a. *L* _____

   b. *M* _____

   c. *N* _____

   d. *P* _____

5. Multiply the numbers in each ordered pair by 3. Write the new ordered pairs.

_____

6. Draw a new figure on the grid using the ordered pairs in exercise 5.

7. Is the figure you drew in exercise 6 congruent to figure *LMNP*? Is the new figure similar to figure *LMNP*?

_____

Name _____

Write the answer.

1. 3267
    − 2100

2. 45)7020

3. 5)16,066

4. 130
    × 52

5. $652.85
    − 196.34

6. 16 min 8 s
    + 10 min 14 s

Write whether each fraction is close to 0, $\frac{1}{2}$, or 1.

7. $\frac{1}{8}$ _____

8. $\frac{15}{16}$ _____

9. $\frac{23}{50}$ _____

Write each fraction as a mixed number in simplest form or as a whole number.

10. $\frac{8}{2}$ _____

11. $\frac{15}{12}$ _____

12. $\frac{27}{10}$ _____

13. $\frac{23}{8}$ _____

14. $\frac{18}{16}$ _____

15. $\frac{7}{3}$ _____

Solve.

16. Victor bought $\frac{1}{4}$ pound of coleslaw, $\frac{3}{4}$ pound of potato salad, and $\frac{1}{2}$ pound of bean salad. How much did his purchases weigh in all?

_____

Name _____

Write the answer in simplest form.

1. $\frac{3}{12} + \frac{5}{12}$ _____

2. $\frac{10}{16} - \frac{3}{16}$ _____

3. $\frac{1}{8} + \frac{1}{8}$ _____

4. $\frac{4}{5} - \frac{1}{5}$ _____

5. $\frac{5}{9} + \frac{4}{9}$ _____

6. $\frac{6}{7} - \frac{4}{7}$ _____

Use the figures to answer each question.

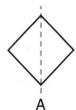
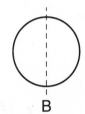

A　　　　　B　　　　　C　　　　　D

7. Which figures have line
symmetry? _____

8. Which figures have half-turn
symmetry? _____

Solve.

9. Monica bought $\frac{3}{4}$ pound of
peanuts. Peter bought $\frac{5}{8}$ pound of
peanuts. Who bought more? _____

10. If peanuts cost $1.59 a pound,
how much would 10 pounds of
peanuts cost? _____

Name _____

Write the answer.

1. $\begin{array}{r} 59 \\ \times\ 27 \\ \hline \end{array}$

2. $\begin{array}{r} \$447.88 \\ 74.23 \\ +\ \ 156.39 \\ \hline \end{array}$

3. $\begin{array}{r} 3.9 \\ -\ 0.453 \\ \hline \end{array}$

4. $80\overline{)3920}$

5. $\begin{array}{r} 0.458 \\ \times\ \ \ \ \ 15 \\ \hline \end{array}$

6. $\begin{array}{r} 76{,}801 \\ +\ 48{,}917 \\ \hline \end{array}$

Write the value of each expression.

7. What is $r + 2$ if $r = 8$? If $r = 20$?   _____

8. What is $18 - s$ if $s = 5$? If $s = 18$?   _____

9. What is $h - 4$ if $h = 9$? If $h = 30$?   _____

10. What is $m + 15$ if $m = 4$? If $m = 9$?   _____

Solve.

11. Fern decorates sweatshirts using plastic
    gems. She sews 40 gems on each
    sweatshirt. How many sweatshirts can she
    decorate with 200 plastic gems?

    _____

Name _____

Write the answer.

1.   84.209
     − 3.031

2.   9.57
     × 0.4

3.   5.03
     + 8.61

4. 2)‾3‾3‾

5. $\frac{1}{4}$
     + $\frac{1}{12}$

6. $\frac{9}{10}$
     − $\frac{1}{5}$

Write the number in standard form.

7. 9 million, 17 thousand   _____

8. 566 thousand, 12   _____

9. 4 billion, 90 million   _____

10. 85 million, 31 thousand, 5   _____

Solve.

11. The president of an office-cleaning business ordered T-shirts with printed logos for her 12 employees. Each shirt cost $5.99 each. There was also a printing charge of $2.00 for each shirt. How much did the order cost in all?

_____

Estimate the answer.

1. $\frac{9}{10} + \frac{1}{12}$ _____

2. $\frac{7}{8} - \frac{2}{7}$ _____

3. $\frac{6}{11} - \frac{7}{20}$ _____

4. $\frac{12}{13} + \frac{5}{6}$ _____

5. $\frac{13}{16} + \frac{5}{12}$ _____

6. $\frac{23}{30} - \frac{2}{9}$ _____

Solve each problem. Use one of the strategies you have learned.

7. Mrs. D'Angelo made a chart of the amount of each type of fabric she has. Which fabric does she have the most of?

Fabric	Amount
Yellow	$3\frac{1}{2}$ yd.
Blue	$7\frac{1}{8}$ yd.
Calico	$5\frac{5}{8}$ yd.
Red Polka Dot	$2\frac{5}{8}$ yd.
Blue Checked	$2\frac{1}{3}$ yd.

_____

8. Does Mrs. D'Angelo have more red polka dot fabric or blue checked fabric? How much more?

_____

9. If Mrs. D'Angelo uses $\frac{1}{2}$ yard of the yellow fabric and $\frac{1}{2}$ yard of the calico fabric to make a blouse for her daughter, how much will she have left of each fabric?

_____

Name _____

Write the answer in simplest form.

1. $3\frac{3}{8}$
     $+ 2\frac{1}{16}$

2. $10\frac{11}{12}$
     $- 2\frac{5}{8}$

3. $6\frac{3}{10}$
     $+ \frac{3}{5}$

4. $5\frac{1}{6} + 2\frac{1}{2}$ _____

5. $3\frac{7}{15} - 1\frac{1}{3}$ _____

6. $4\frac{5}{6} + 4$ _____

7. $1\frac{3}{4} - \frac{1}{8}$ _____

Write the least common multiple.

8. 2, 3, 9 _____

9. 4, 5, 12 _____

10. 3, 10, 20 _____

11. 3, 5, 7 _____

12. 2, 3, 4 _____

13. 3, 4, 5 _____

14. 4, 6, 7 _____

15. 3, 4, 7 _____

Solve.

16. Janell ordered 2 shirts for $16.97 each, a pair of shorts for $19.99, and a belt for $9.50 from a mail-order catalog. The shipping charge was $6.75. How much did her order cost? _____

17. Janell could get next-day delivery of her order for an additional $3.50. How much would her order cost then? _____

Name _____

Write the answer.

1. 4.83
    × 100

2. 4704
    − 1657

3. $7.20
    × 0.5

4. $20.31
    9.77
    + 14.46

5. 6)56.52

6. 18)331

Make each fraction close to $\frac{1}{2}$, but not exactly $\frac{1}{2}$.

7. $\dfrac{3}{\boxed{}}$

8. $\dfrac{8}{\boxed{}}$

9. $\dfrac{\boxed{}}{9}$

10. $\dfrac{\boxed{}}{22}$

11. $\dfrac{\boxed{}}{8}$

12. $\dfrac{6}{\boxed{}}$

Solve.

13. Sue Ann flew nonstop from Baltimore to San Francisco. The flight took 6 hours. She left Baltimore at 7:30 A.M. What time did she arrive in San Francisco? _____

Name _____

Write your estimate.

1. $6 \frac{9}{15} + 2 \frac{4}{9}$ _____

2. $8 \frac{2}{7} - 3 \frac{8}{17}$ _____

3. $4 \frac{9}{14} + 2 \frac{4}{9}$ _____

4. $9 \frac{5}{6} - 5 \frac{9}{10}$ _____

5. $8 \frac{6}{7} + 1 \frac{2}{13}$ _____

6. $10 \frac{3}{16} - \frac{7}{12}$ _____

U.S Standard Time Zone			
9:00 A.M.	10:00 A.M.	11:00 A.M.	12:00 P.M.
San Francisco	Salt Lake City	Minneapolis	Baltimore

Use the time zone table if you need to. Write the time in Minneapolis when it is

7. 4:00 P.M. in San Francisco. _____

8. 8:55 A.M. in Salt Lake City. _____

9. 10:10 P.M. in Baltimore. _____

Solve.

10. If this net is folded into a cube, what number will be opposite the number 6?

_____

11. What number will be opposite the number 1?

_____

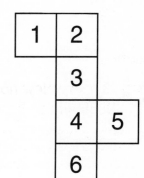

Name _____

Write the answer.

1. 48 min 57 s
  − 22 min 15 s

2. 7 h 26 min
  + 6 h 16 min

3.   69 h 17 min
  − 30 h 9 min

Use the graph to answer each question.

4. How many items are for sale at the Crafts Show?

_____

5. What fraction of the crafts being sold are necklaces?

_____

Items at Craft Sale

5 Aprons
9 Stuffed Animals
4 Necklaces
6 Potholders
12 Wooden Toys

6. What fraction of the crafts are stuffed animals?

_____

7. Do aprons, necklaces, and potholders make up more or less than half of the total items on sale?

_____

8. Which two types of crafts make up half of the items in the crafts sale?

_____

Name _____

Write the answer.

1. 5.5
     × 8

2. 6)10,189

3. 2 h 18 min
     + 2 h 5 min

4. 1.287
     − 0.942

5. 8.75
      4.4
     + 7.58

6. 1.5232 km
     − 0.9421 km

Compare. Write >, <, or =.

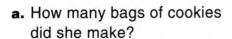

7. $6\frac{1}{8}$ ◯ $5\frac{5}{8}$ **8.** $\frac{5}{6}$ ◯ $\frac{5}{7}$ **9.** $\frac{4}{5}$ ◯ $\frac{8}{10}$

10. $2\frac{2}{15}$ ◯ $2\frac{3}{10}$ **11.** $9\frac{5}{12}$ ◯ $9\frac{7}{8}$ **12.** $5\frac{1}{4}$ ◯ $5\frac{3}{12}$

Solve.

13. Shirley baked 100 cookies for a bake sale.
     She put 3 cookies together in a sandwich
     bag and sold the bags of cookies for $0.25
     each.

   a. How many bags of cookies
        did she make?   _____

   b. If all but 4 bags sold, how much
        money did her cookies bring in
        for the bake sale?   _____

Name _____

Write the compatible numbers you would use to estimate the quotient. Then write the estimate.

1. 6)$2.57 _____

2. 3)$17.10 _____

3. 8)$9.87 _____

4. 9)$0.74 _____

5. 5)$85.49 _____

6. 7)$80.37 _____

Estimate the amount saved on each item.

7. Sofa for $829 with $\frac{1}{10}$ off _____

8. Pair of roller skates for $39.00 with $\frac{1}{4}$ off _____

9. Telephone for $24.00 with $\frac{1}{5}$ off _____

10. Set of encyclopedias for $349 with $\frac{1}{6}$ off _____

11. Jacket for $59.98 with $\frac{1}{3}$ off _____

12. Hat for $17.50 with $\frac{1}{4}$ off _____

DAILY CUMULATIVE REVIEW

Write the answer.

1. 79
    × 79

2. 65$\overline{)2206}$

3. 5$\overline{)6065}$

4. 513
    × 7

5. 928,161
    + 53,899

6. 82,647
    − 9,660

Write the missing angle measure for each triangle.

7. △STV   ∠S = 72°   ∠T = 36°   ∠V = _____

8. △GHI   ∠G = 85°   ∠H = 25°   ∠I = _____

9. △XYZ   ∠X = 107°   ∠Y = 53°   ∠Z = _____

10. △PQR   ∠P = 29°   ∠Q = 78°   ∠R = _____

Solve.

11. At the market, 6 apples sell for $1.00 and 6 oranges sell for $1.50. Sumiyo has $0.50. Does she have enough money to buy 1 apple and 1 orange?

_____

Name _____

Add or subtract. Use mental math.

1. 80 + 70 = _____

2. 900 − 450 = _____

3. 300 + 4000 = _____

4. 600 − 199 = _____

5. 39 + 62 = _____

6. $40.00 − $9.99 = _____

7. 50 + 30 + 10 + 20 = _____

Write the mean, median, and range for each set of data.

8. 976, 487, 501, 734, 648, 812

_____

9. 78, 66, 84, 90, 82

_____

10. 90°, 85°, 92°, 84°, 78°, 81°

_____

Solve.

11. On Saturday, Derrick must leave for work at noon. Before he goes to work he wants to have 45 minutes for breakfast, 2 hours to work in the garden, and $\frac{1}{2}$ hour to get ready to go to work. What time does Derrick need to get up? _____

Name _____

Write the answer.

1. $4\frac{1}{5}$
$+ 1\frac{2}{3}$

2. $14\frac{1}{10}$
$- 5\frac{7}{10}$

3. $5\frac{1}{2}$
$+ \frac{3}{8}$

4. $3 \times \frac{1}{9}$ _____

5. $7\frac{7}{12} - 1\frac{1}{12}$ _____

6. $\frac{3}{4} \times 6$ _____

7. $\frac{1}{2} \times \frac{1}{5}$ _____

Write each number as a decimal.

8. $\frac{1}{25}$ _____

9. $\frac{61}{100}$ _____

10. $\frac{3}{20}$ _____

Solve.

11. Tiffany is on the cross-country track team. On Wednesday she ran $8\frac{1}{4}$ miles. How many quarter miles did she run?

_____

12. The student council wants to serve lasagna at the faculty appreciation lunch. Each lasagna casserole makes 6 servings. If 20 teachers each have 1 serving, how many lasagna casseroles will the council have to prepare?

_____

142 DAILY CUMULATIVE REVIEW

Use the number line to find each quotient.

1. $4 \div \frac{2}{3} =$ _____

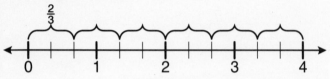

2. $3 \div \frac{1}{6} =$ _____

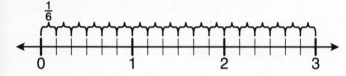

3. $5 \div \frac{5}{8} =$ _____

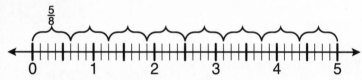

4. $4 \div \frac{2}{5} =$ _____

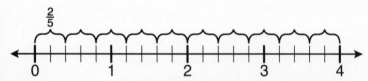

Round each number to the greatest place.

5. 651 _____   **6.** 4.71 _____   **7.** 70.82 _____

8. $2430 _____   **9.** 628 _____   **10.** 95.42 _____

143 DAILY CUMULATIVE REVIEW

Write the answer.

1. $\frac{1}{10} + \frac{3}{10}$ _____

2. $0.972 \div 0.9$ _____

3. 1.51×20 _____

4. $3 \div 4$ _____

5. $\frac{11}{12} - \frac{7}{12}$ _____

6. 0.3×5.92 _____

**Use the figures to answer each question.
You may use tracing paper.**

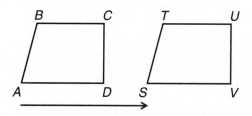
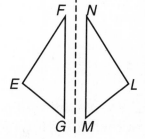

7. $\angle BAD$ in figure *ABCD* is congruent to which angle in slide image *STUV*?

_____

8. $\overline{CD}$ in figure *ABCD* is congruent to which segment in the slide image *STUV*?

_____

9. $\overline{FG}$ in $\triangle EFG$ is congruent to which segment in the flip image?

_____

10. $\angle FEG$ in $\triangle EFG$ is congruent to which angle in the flip image?

_____

144 DAILY CUMULATIVE REVIEW

Write the product in simplest form.

1. $\frac{4}{7} \times \frac{1}{3} =$ _____

2. $\frac{2}{3} \times 9 =$ _____

3. $\frac{2}{5} \times \frac{1}{4} =$ _____

4. $\frac{2}{5} \times \frac{2}{3} =$ _____

5. $8 \times \frac{1}{8} =$ _____

6. $\frac{1}{6} \times \frac{3}{4} =$ _____

Write the first three common multiples.

7. 6, 9 _____

8. 5, 9 _____

9. 2, 3, 5 _____

10. 5, 7, 14 _____

**Solve. If there is not enough information,
tell what information is needed.**

11. Pablo takes care of his little brother after
school. His mother pays him $2 an hour.

    a. If Pablo starts taking care of his brother at
3:00 P.M. on school days, how much
money does he earn each day?

_____

    b. On Saturday, Pablo earned $10 watching
his brother. How many hours did he work?

_____

145 DAILY CUMULATIVE REVIEW

Write your estimate.

1. $41.06
     − $7.19

2. 5162
     + 9189

3. 298
     ×   4

4. 8) 3898

5. 239
      38
    + 480

6. 2046
     − 648

Write the perimeter of each polygon.

7.

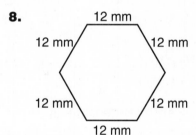

12 ft
12 ft | 12 ft
12 ft

8.

12 mm
12 mm / 12 mm
12 mm \ 12 mm
12 mm

_____   _____

9.

50 m
20 m

10.

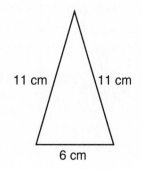

11 cm / 11 cm
6 cm

_____   _____

DAILY CUMULATIVE REVIEW

Write the product. Round dollar amounts to the nearest cent.

1. $7.98
× 6.4

2. 391
× 0.08

3. $4.82
× 31

4. $0.54 × 2.9 = _____

5. 744.5 × 0.5 = _____

6. 4.62 × 4.9 = _____

7. $6.19 × 2.7 = _____

Write each mixed number as an equivalent fraction.

8. $5\frac{5}{6}$ _____

9. $3\frac{1}{10}$ _____

10. $2\frac{11}{15}$ _____

11. $7\frac{2}{9}$ _____

12. $1\frac{1}{3}$ _____

13. $8\frac{3}{5}$ _____

Solve. Use guess and check and make a table, or use other strategies you think will help.

14. Wei-Hsiu helps his father sell rings and necklaces at craft fairs. The rings sell for $9.50 each and the necklaces sell for $17 each. On Saturday they sold the same number of each item and their total sales were $265. How many rings did they sell? _____

Name _____

Write the answer. Use mental math.

1. $900 \times 80 =$ _____

2. $4.12 \times 10 =$ _____

3. $2000 \div 20 =$ _____

4. $1170 \div 10 =$ _____

5. $0.728 \times 100 =$ _____

6. $300 \times 50 =$ _____

7. $54{,}000 \div 900 =$ _____

8. $150 \div 1000 =$ _____

Write each whole or mixed number as a fraction. Then write its reciprocal.

9. $2\frac{5}{12}$ _____

10. 6 _____

11. $3\frac{1}{2}$ _____

12. $3\frac{7}{10}$ _____

Solve.

13. A recipe for carrot spice muffins includes $1\frac{1}{2}$ cups grated carrots and the following spices: $\frac{1}{4}$ teaspoon of nutmeg, $\frac{1}{2}$ teaspoon cinnamon, $\frac{1}{8}$ teaspoon allspice.

a. What is the total amount of spices called for in the recipe?

_____

b. To double the recipe, how much grated carrot is needed?

_____

Name _____

···

Write the answer.

1. 613
   × 97

2. 6)1860

3. 39)6008

4. 875,372
   − 18,785

5. 764
   × 235

6. $20.90
     15.36
   + 2.73

**Write *prime* or *composite* for each number.
If the number is composite, give its prime
factorization.**

7. 42 _____

8. 99 _____

9. 63 _____

10. 101 _____

Solve.

11. Irene's height was $48\frac{1}{2}$ inches
last year. Today she measures
$49\frac{3}{4}$ inches tall. How much did
she grow in the past year?   _____

149 DAILY CUMULATIVE REVIEW

Write the answer in simplest form.

1. $7\frac{1}{6}$
$+ 2\frac{3}{4}$

2. $10\frac{7}{9}$
$- 5\frac{1}{2}$

3. $8\frac{9}{16}$
$+ \frac{1}{2}$

4. $3\frac{5}{6}$
$- 2$

5. $4\frac{3}{8}$
$+ 3\frac{3}{8}$

6. $6\frac{1}{5}$
$- \frac{7}{10}$

7. $\frac{7}{10} + \frac{4}{15} =$ _____

8. $\frac{9}{16} - \frac{1}{4} =$ _____

Write each fraction as a decimal.

9. $\frac{3}{10}$ _____

10. $\frac{21}{25}$ _____

11. $\frac{437}{1000}$ _____

Solve.

12. Kim lives $\frac{9}{10}$ mile from the zoo. Yolanda lives $\frac{5}{8}$ mile from the zoo. Who lives closer to the zoo?

_____

13. Mrs. Ling walked $\frac{1}{4}$ mile from her home to the supermarket. Then she walked home with the groceries. How far did she walk in all?

_____

Name _____

Write your estimate.

1. $9\frac{1}{10} + 5\frac{6}{7}$ _____

2. $\frac{2}{15} + \frac{1}{12}$ _____

3. $6\frac{4}{5} - 2\frac{1}{6}$ _____

4. $\frac{8}{9} - \frac{7}{18}$ _____

5. $2\frac{5}{16} + \frac{10}{11}$ _____

6. $8\frac{3}{5} - \frac{7}{8}$ _____

Write how much time will pass.

7. from 5:00 P.M. to 6:39 P.M. _____

8. from 7:45 A.M. to 8:20 A.M. _____

9. from 2:40 A.M. to 6:00 A.M. _____

10. from 1:15 P.M. to 7:00 P.M. _____

Solve.

11. Rosalind jogs on the $\frac{1}{5}$-mile track at the Stay Fit Health Club. Jesse jogs on the $\frac{1}{3}$-mile track at Oceanview Park.

    a. Rosalind jogs 8 times around the track. Write the total distance she jogs as a fraction and as a mixed number. _____

    b. If Rosalind and Jesse each run 12 laps at their jogging tracks, who has run farther? _____

Name _____

Write the answer in simplest form.

1. $\frac{5}{6} \times \frac{1}{2} =$ _____

2. $\frac{1}{4} \times \frac{3}{8} =$ _____

3. $9 \div \frac{3}{8} =$ _____

4. $10 \div \frac{2}{5} =$ _____

5. $\frac{7}{10} \times 5 =$ _____

6. $12 \div \frac{3}{4} =$ _____

Complete.

7. 692 m = _____ km

8. 36 mm = _____ m

9. 130 cm = _____ mm

10. 27 cm = _____ m

Read each story. Does the underlined sentence make sense? Explain.

11. Marvin walked 2 miles to the beach. Jamie walked $1\frac{3}{4}$ miles to meet Marvin at the beach. <u>Marvin arrived first.</u>

_____

_____

12. The arts-and-crafts center is open from 3:00 P.M. to 5:00 P.M. <u>Jack, Patrice, and Megan each were at the center at different times. They were each there for 1 hour.</u>

_____

_____

Name _____

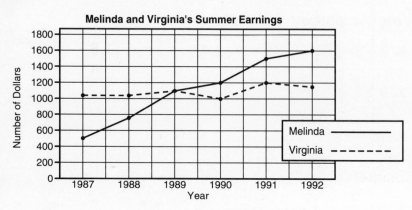

Melinda and Virginia's Summer Earnings

Use the graph to answer each question.

1. In which year did Melinda and Virginia earn the same amount? _____

2. Whose summer income changed the least over the years shown on the graph? _____

3. In which year did they have the greatest difference in their summer incomes? _____

4. About how much did Melinda earn in 1987? _____

5. Write *a*, *b*, or *c*. The graph shows that Melinda's summer income has generally
   a. been increasing.
   b. remained the same.
   c. been decreasing. _____

153 DAILY CUMULATIVE REVIEW

Write the answer.

1.   3.9 cm
      1.8 cm
  + 6.5 cm

2.   10.044
   − 8.627

3.   1.8
   ×   8

4. 9)$19.17

5.   79.627
      4.983
  + 17.408

6. $1.45
   ×   7.2

Write each ratio three different ways.

7. stars to diamonds

_____

8. hearts to total shapes

_____

9. diamonds to hearts

_____

Solve.

10. There are 15 boys in a class of 27 students. Write the ratio of girls to boys three different ways.

_____

Name _____

Write the answer.

1. 4.20
    ×   8

2. 0.67
    × 0.7

3. 3.99
    × 1.8

4. 5⟌42

5. 4⟌$10.80

6. 7⟌7.056

What point does each ordered pair below name?

7. (1,3)   _____

8. (3,1)   _____

9. (5,3)   _____

10. (3,3)   _____

11. (5,2)   _____

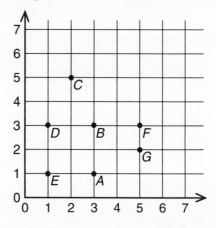

Solve.

12. Alice brought 2 loaves of pumpkin bread for refreshments at the Photography Club meeting. Each loaf was cut into 10 slices. All but 2 slices were eaten. Write a mixed number to describe the amount that was eaten.

_____

155 DAILY CUMULATIVE REVIEW

Write the answer in simplest form.

1. $12\frac{7}{8}$
$-\ 6\frac{1}{6}$

2. $4\frac{5}{9}$
$+\ \frac{1}{3}$

3. $\frac{9}{10}$
$-\ \frac{1}{4}$

4. $\frac{5}{16} + \frac{8}{16}$ _____

5. $6\frac{7}{12} + 7$ _____

6. $\frac{1}{9} \times \frac{2}{3}$ _____

7. $\frac{2}{5} \times \frac{5}{8}$ _____

Write each percent as a decimal and as a fraction in simplest form.

8. 40% _____

9. 7% _____

10. 55% _____

11. 90% _____

12. 75% _____

13. 65% _____

14. 80% _____

15. 5% _____

Solve.

16. Lamont had $10. He spent 40% of his money to see a movie. How much did he spend on the movie?

_____

17. Leora had $20. She spent 40% of her money on a cassette. How much did she spend on the cassette?

_____

Write the answer. Use mental math.

1. 25% of 16 _____ **2.** 50% of 60 _____

3. 50% of 20 _____ **4.** 25% of 12 _____

5. 25% of 360 _____ **6.** 50% of 120 _____

7. 50% of 80 _____ **8.** 25% of 400 _____

Complete to make equivalent fractions.

9. $\frac{2}{5} = \frac{\square}{20}$ **10.** $\frac{3}{7} = \frac{6}{\square}$ **11.** $\frac{8}{\square} = \frac{3}{3}$

12. $\frac{\square}{27} = \frac{2}{9}$ **13.** $\frac{3}{9} = \frac{\square}{27}$ **14.** $\frac{7}{\square} = \frac{21}{30}$

15. $\frac{8}{12} = \frac{\square}{3}$ **16.** $\frac{5}{8} = \frac{15}{\square}$ **17.** $\frac{7}{\square} = \frac{5}{5}$

Solve.

18. Mr. Arroyo is buying a book. The regular price is $25. The sale price is $\frac{1}{5}$ off the regular price. How much money will Mr. Arroyo save by buying the book on sale? _____

157 DAILY CUMULATIVE REVIEW

Write the product in simplest form.

1. $\frac{2}{5} \times \frac{1}{8}$ _____

2. $\frac{1}{4} \times \frac{1}{4}$ _____

3. $2 \times \frac{7}{12}$ _____

4. $\frac{2}{3} \times \frac{1}{6}$ _____

5. $\frac{5}{6} \times \frac{3}{10}$ _____

6. $\frac{5}{7} \times \frac{3}{5}$ _____

7. $\frac{3}{4} \times \frac{4}{9}$ _____

8. $\frac{2}{3} \times 6$ _____

Write the answer.

9. $25 - 5 \div (4 + 1)$ _____

10. $18 \div (3 + 3) + 7$ _____

11. $4 \times 3 + 4$ _____

12. $3 + (4 + 4) \cdot 4$ _____

Solve. Making notes may help you.

13. Robin is twice as old as her sister and 3 years younger than her brother, who is 9 years old. How old is Robin's sister?

_____

14. Ellen left her house at 9:00 A.M. Two hours later she stopped at her friend's house where she visited for $1\frac{1}{2}$ hours. Together they walked for 10 minutes to the library. Ellen stayed at the library for 3 hours and 15 minutes. She then walked home in 5 minutes. What time did she arrive home?

_____

158 DAILY CUMULATIVE REVIEW

Write the answer. Use mental math.

1. 32 cm + 48 cm = _____   **2.** 7342 − 999 = _____

3. 50 + 30 + 20 = _____   **4.** 200 × 50 = _____

5. 36,000 ÷ 60 = _____   **6.** 8500 − 2500 = _____

7. $1.99 × 5 = _____   **8.** 900 ÷ 30 = _____

Compare. Write <, >, or =.

9. 3.4 ◯ 3.04   **10.** $\frac{8}{12}$ ◯ $\frac{16}{24}$

11. 0.389 ◯ 0.398   **12.** $1\frac{4}{5}$ ◯ $\frac{9}{5}$

13. 5.7 ◯ 7.05   **14.** 0.634 ◯ 0.436

Solve. Use a word equation when it helps.

15. Emily made a small batch of trail mix using 1 cup of raisins and 2 cups of peanuts. If she uses 16 cups of peanuts to make another batch, how many cups of raisins should she use?

16. Ralph's mother gave him $25 to buy some groceries and a new sweatshirt. He spent $8.95 on the sweatshirt and $12.38 on the groceries. How much money did he have left?

_____   _____

DAILY CUMULATIVE REVIEW

Write the compatible numbers you would use to estimate the quotient. Then write the estimate.

1. $7\overline{)\$1.30}$ _____

2. $9\overline{)\$0.39}$ _____

3. $6\overline{)\$4.17}$ _____

4. $8\overline{)\$24.79}$ _____

5. $4\overline{)\$288.70}$ _____

6. $5\overline{)\$45.48}$ _____

Write each probability in the form of a ratio.

7. If you cover your eyes and pick a card, what is the probability of choosing a card with a heart on it?

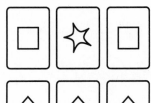

_____

8. What is the probability of choosing a card with a star or a heart?

_____

9. What is the probability of choosing a card with a circle on it?

_____

10. Is there a greater chance of choosing a card with a square on it or a card with a diamond on it?

_____

DAILY CUMULATIVE REVIEW

Write the answer in simplest form.

1. $3\frac{1}{3}$
   $+ 3\frac{1}{6}$

2. $7\frac{3}{16}$
   $- 4$

3. $5\frac{5}{12}$
   $+ 2\frac{3}{8}$

4. $6\frac{1}{8} - 2\frac{1}{2}$ _____

5. $\frac{3}{7} + \frac{2}{7}$ _____

6. $\frac{4}{5} - \frac{7}{15}$ _____

7. $1\frac{1}{4} + \frac{3}{5}$ _____

Decide if the ratios are equal. Write *yes* or *no*.

8. 4:2 and 8:1 _____

9. 9 to 10 and 18 to 20 _____

10. $\frac{7}{6}$ and $\frac{21}{18}$ _____

11. 5 to 12 and 12 to 5 _____

12. 2:6 and 3:9 _____

13. 9 to 6 and 2 to 3 _____

Solve. Use guess and check and make a table, or use other strategies you think will help.

14. Pete and Jeff sold a total of 18 bags of either popcorn or peanuts at a school game. They want to know how many of each were sold. Popcorn sold for 25¢ a bag and peanuts sold for 40¢ a bag. The boys started with $5.50 in change and ended up with $11.50. How many bags of popcorn and how many bags of peanuts did they sell?

_____

Name _____

Write the answer.

1. 2 h 31 min
　　+ 3 h　7 min

2. 6 h 29 min
　　− 2 h　5 min

3. 48 h 26 min
　　+ 16 h 19 min

4. 8 min 36 s
　　− 5 min 17 s

5. 30 min 10 s
　　+ 17 min 36 s

6. 47 min 39 s
　　− 25 min 18 s

Write the letter of the most reasonable estimate for the shaded part.

7.
　　a. 10%
　　b. 50%
　　c. 60%

　　_____

8.
　　a. 2%
　　b. 10%
　　c. 20%

　　_____

9.
　　a. 20%
　　b. 5%
　　c. 50%

　　_____

10.
　　a. 100%
　　b. 80%
　　c. 95%

　　_____

Solve.

11. Last year, Mr. Costello planted
10 tomato plants. Of these,
7 plants lived through the
summer. What percent of the
plants died?

　　　　　　　　_____

Name _____

162 DAILY CUMULATIVE REVIEW

Write the answer.

1. $40.14
   23.35
+ 8.90

2. 1.561
− 0.793

3. 6.5
× 8

4. 9)90.27

5. 1.01
× 2.7

6. 8)$14.40

Write the missing number.

7. 3 × $4.32   Estimate: between $12 and $ _____

8. 4 × $6.89   Estimate: between $ _____ and $28

9. 8 × 1.6   Estimate: between _____ and _____

10. 9 × 4.93   Estimate: between _____ and _____

Solve.

11. Greg earns $9.50 for each hour he works as
a handyman. If he works 7 hours, will he
earn more or less than $70?

_____

Name _____

Write the answer. Use mental math.

1. $9.66 \times 10 =$ _____

2. $1.85 \div 10 =$ _____

3. $51.4 \times 100 =$ _____

4. $0.88 \div 100 =$ _____

5. $19.32 \times 1000 =$ _____

6. $84.9 \div 1000 =$ _____

7. $204.4 \times 10 =$ _____

8. $4.81 \div 100 =$ _____

Estimate the area. Give your answer in square units.

9.
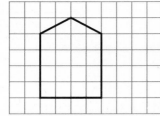

_____

10.
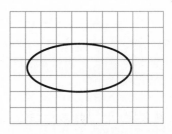

_____

11.
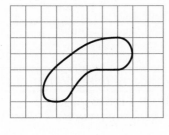

_____

12.
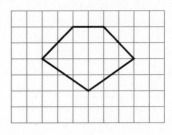

_____

DAILY CUMULATIVE REVIEW

Write the answer in simplest form.

1. $\frac{1}{2} \times \frac{5}{12}$ _____   **2.** $5 \div \frac{1}{5}$ _____

3. $4 \div \frac{1}{2}$ _____   **4.** $\frac{3}{10} \times 5$ _____

5. $\frac{3}{4} \times \frac{7}{8}$ _____   **6.** $7 \div \frac{7}{16}$ _____

Write the decimal as a fraction or mixed number in simplest form.

7. 3.6 _____   **8.** 6.07 _____   **9.** 0.65 _____

10. 1.36 _____   **11.** 5.75 _____   **12.** 0.3 _____

Complete the word equation. Use it to solve the problem.

13. Caleb is hiking a 12-mile trail. He started at 8:00 A.M. and had hiked the first 2 miles by 8:45 A.M. If he keeps going at the same speed, when will he be finished? _____

ratio of miles to minutes for first part of trail	=	ratio of miles to minutes for whole trail

$$\frac{\text{miles in first part}}{\text{minutes in first part}} = \boxed{}$$

Name _____

Write the percent of the number. Use mental math when you can.

1. 60% of 300 _____   **2.** 3% of 280 _____

3. 19% of 450 _____   **4.** 90% of 200 _____

5. 44% of 150 _____   **6.** 50% of 160 _____

7. 11% of 100 _____   **8.** 75% of 272 _____

Write the area of each rectangle. Remember to use square units in your answer.

9.

15 cm
2.5 cm

_____

10.

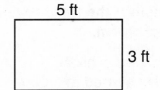

5 ft
3 ft

_____

11.

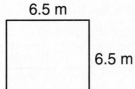

6.5 m
6.5 m

_____

12.

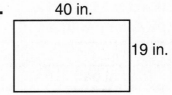

40 in.
19 in.

_____

Name _____

 166 **DAILY CUMULATIVE REVIEW**
....

Write the answer.

1. 27.167
     + 9.056

2.   827,355
     − 359,073

3.   8.39
     × 100

4. 5$\overline{)14}$

5. 2$\frac{1}{7}$
     + 1$\frac{3}{7}$

6.   7
     − 3$\frac{2}{3}$

Write the answer. Write whether you used mental math or paper and pencil.

7. 6.08 × 9.7 _____

8. 490 ÷ 7 _____

9. 10% of 90 _____

10. 4.16 + 69.27 _____

11. $\frac{3}{8} \times \frac{1}{2}$ _____

12. 25% of 800 _____

13. Tony buys a compact disc for $11.99. He pays for it with a $10 bill and a $5 bill. How much change does he receive?

_____

14. A calculator is on sale for 30% off. The regular price is $29.00. How much is saved by buying the calculator on sale?

_____